FO
FR

EASTERN REGION FREIGHT
SINCE 1960

FOCUS ON
FREIGHT

EASTERN REGION FREIGHT
SINCE 1960

Shaun Pearce

First published 1995

ISBN 0 7110 2345 X

Published by Ian Allan Publishing

an imprint of Ian Allan Ltd, Terminal House, Station Approach, Shepperton, Surrey TW17 8AS.
Printed by Ian Allan Printing Ltd, Coombelands House, Coombelands Lane, Addlestone, Weybridge, Surrey KT15 1HY.

Front cover: **Class 37 No 37087 with the Stratford Market trip, Temple Mills, 4 July 1989.** *Paul D. Shannon*

Back cover top: **Class 08 shunter No 08531 with fuel tanks for the depot, Ripple Lane, 4 July 1989.**

Back cover bottom: **An unidentified Class 40 with the Whitemoor-Parkeston Quay freight on 31 May 1979.** *John D. Mannion*

Half title page: **Class O2 2-8-0 No 63951 passes with an up freight.** *John C. Baker*

Title page:
'A4' Pacific No 60030 *Golden Fleece* heads a fast freight north of Potters Bar on 28 September 1960. *R. Southam*

Contents page: **Just about everything went by rail at some time or another. This picture illustrates that point well! Class 40 No 40029 *Saxonia* nears Thurston with a Whitemoor-Parkeston air-braked service on 19 June 1978.** *John C. Baker*

Introduction page: **Class 08 shunter No 08257 brings malt, in polythene bags, from the Associated British Maltsters sidings into the goods yard on 28 September 1982.** *John C. Baker*

Contents

Acknowledgements

I would like to express my sincere thanks and appreciation to everyone who responded to my requests for information, especially the following: Dick Crane, at Railfreight Distribution, for giving me access to his archive; John T. Gibson, at Butterley Brick, and R. E. Hailey, John Allison, and Mick Moore, at British Sugar, for allowing me to reproduce the blueprints of their companies' rail connections; John Collier, at National Power, for the information about West Burton pokwer station; Ted Burke, at Esso, A. M. Taylor, at Foster Yeoman, D. R. George, at ABP King's Lynn, R. R. Aspinal, at the Museum of London/Museum in Docklands, Bill Hollowell, at the British Sugar Beet Review, and Barbara Morris, at the Newmarket Racecourses Trust, for their valuable contributions.

Thanks also to the staff at the Ashford Public Library, Ashford, Kent for their help and assistance.

Last, but by no means least, I would like to thank Paul Shannon and John Baker for not only being able to provide many of the pictures that I was looking for, but also for suggesting locations and traffic types that I would not have otherwise considered.

Shaun Pearce

Introduction

Freight used to be the bread and butter of the railways. The movement of manufactured goods, raw materials, livestock and coal made railway expansion possible — as for the canals that the railways superseded — and kept passenger fares low. The public, however, saw very little of this. Goods trains ran during off-peak times and at night. Goods traffic was very unglamorous, and was conducted away from public view. The public had, therefore, little occasion to explore the areas set aside specifically for freight — except when their passenger trains skirted the big rail yards that existed on the outskirts of major cities.

The years between 1960 and 1990 saw perhaps greater changes in the handling of freight than at any other period in the history of the railways. Steam traction gave way to electric and diesel, and the whole system of handling freight changed dramatically — until most freight traffic was abandoned altogether.

Traditional wagonload freight workings were refined into the new air-braked Speedlink services. Block trains of one product from one place

directly to another became the norm. The whole idea of freight by rail was shaken up by the Serpell Report, and Section 8 grants encouraged companies who had never thought of using rail for distribution to get on track.

Time and space permit only a brief overview of all this to be represented here. For readers wishing to explore this subject in more depth, there are many places to look. Some are listed at the back of this book.

The book is mostly photographic. The photographs have been arranged into broad categories by location and traffic type. It is possible, however, that a particular photograph could be equally at home in more than one section — this is particularly true of Speedlink services.

Note:
British Rail 'went metric' on 30 December 1973. In this book all statistics generated before that date are in imperial weights and measures; those generated afterwards are in metric. To convert tons to tonnes multiply by 1.016.

The pick-up goods train was once a familiar sight on the railways of Britain. Here 'J17' 0-6-0 No 64646 arrives at Bury St Edmunds with the daily pick-up goods from Sudbury in May 1961. *John C. Baker*

Below: In 1960 BR tried to impress its fast freight customers by naming some express freight trains. The first was the 'Lea Valley Enterprise' from Tottenham to Whitemoor via the Great Eastern Line. This was soon followed by the 'East Essex Enterprise' from Chelmsford and Colchester to the Midlands and North. In this picture, the latter passes Thurston in May 1960 *en route* for Whitemoor — hauled by Class 31 No D5538. *John C. Baker*

Focus on Freight

Overview

The way railway freight was handled had evolved over time as railways grew and expanded. Goods would be brought to a railhead — either at a factory or private siding, or by road to a station goods yard — where they would be loaded on to a wagon. The necessary paperwork would be completed, and the wagonload of goods collected by a pick-up goods train. The pick-up goods train would make its way to a large rail yard, stopping to pick-up or drop off wagons at other sidings *en route*. At the yard, the wagon would be marshalled into a mixed goods train which would then set off in the general direction of the wagon's eventual destination. The train might call at other marshalling yards along the way, where the wagon could be marshalled into other trains. The process would repeat itself until the wagon was in a yard nearest to its destination. From there, a pick-up goods train would take it the rest of the way to a private siding or station goods yard, where it would be unloaded. Even a comparatively short journey could take several days, the bulk of which would be spent in yards waiting to be shunted. This was no problem when roads were poor, but as motorways were built — and the capacity of lorries began to grow — the railways began to face serious competition.

The years covered by this book, 1960-1990, saw arguably the greatest changes in the way railway freight was handled since nationalisation. The first instrument of change was the Transport Act of 1962. Under this Act, the British Transport Commission (the statutory body that had overseen transport since 1948) was dissolved. Each area of transport — road, rail, waterways, etc — was given its own autonomy. For rail freight this meant the end of forced co-operation with British Road Services, thus setting up direct competition for long distance traffic that had not existed before. The newly-created British Railways Board was also absolved of its duty to act as a common carrier, thereby permitting it to turn away business it did not deem profitable.

The same year also saw the National Sundries Plan formulated. This was intended to rationalise the sundries traffic or 'smalls' — an area of declining traffic and rising costs. Goods depots were grouped into three broad categories: Main, Secondary and Auxiliary. Main depots handled substantial tonnages and were served by direct trains. Secondary depots had some direct trains, but only where traffic was sufficient. Auxiliary depots were mostly local road collection and delivery sidings. This plan ensured that 70% of sundries traffic went direct from one main depot to another.

In 1963, a reshaping report was commissioned. One of the points it raised was the high cost of the wagon fleet, and how poorly it was utilised. A central wagon authority was set up to co-ordinate wagon movements, but as the Beeching studies branded wagonload freight a loss-maker, it became clear that BR would have to undertake some radical changes.

One of the first changes was the adoption of block trains. A block train carries just a single commodity, from one destination directly to another. Industries such as oil and coal were the first to benefit from this concept — as were large manufacturing companies such as Ford, which was able to use trains to move components and finished products from one factory to another. An offshoot of the block train idea, Merry-go-round, was devised to supply coal to the new coal-fired power stations in the East Midlands and elsewhere.

The adoption of Freightliners in the 'container revolution' also dramatically changed the face of railway freight operations. The concept was a simple one: put as many cargoes as possible into standard-sized metal boxes, put these metal boxes on to block trains from dedicated terminal to dedicated terminal, then transfer them to lorries for distribution to the customer. This concept, perhaps more than anything else, had the greatest impact on railway freight operations during the 1960s.

With so many block trains running, the marshalling yards — long the 'hubs' of the network — were being bypassed and becoming rapidly outdated. Many were rebuilt, others abandoned, but most were retained (for the time being) to cope with the not inconsiderable amount of wagonload freight still on the network. The

Left: **A wide variety of goods wagons can be seen in Ipswich yard as No D1760 hauls the 14.20 Norwich-Liverpool Street past East Suffolk Junction signalbox on 30 April 1966.** *G. R. Mortimer*

Left: **Computers were used — in a big way — to keep track of individual wagons and containers, enabling them to be rostered more efficiently.** *Courtesy Railfreight Distribution*

Below: **The wagon repair shop at Immingham on 25 September 1987.** *Brian Morrison*

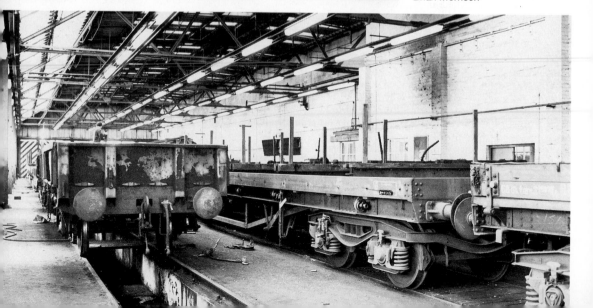

National Freight Train Plan of 1965 reorganised them into Primary and Secondary yards as part of a streamlining operation.

The National Freight Plan of 1965 was also designed to improve train loading, reduce line occupation and make working practices more efficient.

Throughout the 1960s and 1970s, BR and the government tried various ways of maximising revenue from freight operations. The Transport Act of 1968 set about restructuring the wagonload business as a strictly disciplined, viable operation. Investment was curbed, and an emphasis put on flexibility and getting more out of existing assets. Long term contracts were deemed more important than short term 'marginal' traffic. BR opted out of carrying some types of freight if they were thought to be unremunerative, and unproductive sidings were closed. BR's Freight Plan of 1971 reversed this thinking slightly, recognising that short term business was necessary to keep up cash flow.

With the diversity of freight traffic on the Eastern Region, these changes began to pay off. In 1969, for example, the Region offset the loss of a million tons of coal traffic due to a miners' strike, with an improvement of around the same amount in iron and steel movements. The carriage of petroleum products grew as the refineries in the Immingham area came on stream. By 1971, more freight was originating on the Eastern Region than any other. It was expected that by 1976 the Region would generate 98 million tons of freight — around 48% of the entire system's traffic.

BR adopted the Total Operations Processing System (TOPS) for wagonload freight. The system, devised in 1972, went 'on line' in the Eastern Region on 27 October 1975. TOPS — originally developed in the USA by the Southern Pacific Railroad — was a computer-based system, capable of continuously monitoring, recording and reporting every detail of freight traffic on the network. This allowed highly efficient use of all wagons as the computer knew the location of each wagon at any given moment. So efficient was the system that by 1976, customers could even get information about their wagons by Telex. Empty wagons were given the same treatment as full ones, so the practice of empty wagons accumulating in marshalling yards to await dispersal was eliminated. The computer could also calculate weight and brake force, and thereby facilitate more efficient loading and use of motive power. COPS, a container version of TOPS, was brought on line in 1979. This made for more efficient container handling.

Each type of wagon was given a letter coding and a number. Companies were encouraged to own their own wagons. By 1978, it was estimated that private owner wagons were carrying 30% of all cargoes. Many wagons were foreign, reflecting the important connections to Europe via Harwich and other train-ferry equipped ports.

A sharp downturn in the economy during the early 1970s was reflected in a decrease in tonnage moved by rail. It was claimed in 1975 that rail was carrying only 20% of the country's inland freight. A new BR subsidiary company, Speedlink, was designed to streamline the remaining wagonload business and attract new customers. It was launched in 1977.

Another factor designed to stop the decline of railway freight operations, and which in turn made Speedlink possible, was the Railways Act of 1974. Under Section 8 of that Act, the government would give grants to companies to establish rail links to their premises. The criteria were strict. Grants were given only where there would be benefits to the local environment, and where without help road transport would be used instead of rail. These grants could be for as much as 50% of the cost. This figure was later raised to 60% and the scheme extended to cover privately-owned wagons. East Anglia and the southeast were the largest beneficiaries.

The 'Winter of Discontent' of 1978/79 caused massive problems for BR's freight sector. A 13-week strike at British Steel cost BR nearly £13 million in lost revenue. There was a shortage of motive power, and BR was forced to turn away business. Many customers changed to road haulage and stayed there. Their motto seemed to be 'a friend during an industrial dispute is a friend indeed'.

An intensive marketing campaign in the early 1980s won back some of the bulk grain and domestic coal traffic previously lost to road haulage. Aggregates traffic also benefited from the building boom of the late 1970s and early 1980s. BR developed a new commercial strategy for dealing with its remaining wagonload traffic. Put simply, anything that could not be converted to block train or Speedlink working would be discarded. In 1984 conventional wagonload traffic ended altogether and the system of freight handling described at the beginning of this section was consigned to the history books. The big marshalling yards would eventually be closed and sold off.

The Serpell Report on Railway Finances of 1983 had important ramifications for freight. It applauded the development of Speedlink, but was sceptical of BR's forecasts about its growth. It was pessimistic about the prospects for the involvement of more private capital in rail freight operation — something the government was keen on at the time. It was also concerned that freight was not paying enough towards track signalling costs, and that substantial savings could be made in other engineering costs associated with freight operations. Driver-only freight trains and other changes to traditional working practices to increase productivity were also recommended. Most of its recommendations were carried out in the years that followed.

Speedlink and freightliner were merged in the 1980s to form a single freight sector — Railfreight Distribution. This was divided into six subsectors: Coal, Construction, Metals & Automotive, Petroleum, Speedlink Distribution and Railfreight International. Network Coal, which handled domestic solid fuel, had originally been included in Speedlink. As demand fell the commitment to yard processing required by Speedlink could not be justified and the business was closed.

As 1990 dawned, freight operations on BR bore little resemblance to what had been the norm in 1960. Gone were the big yards and station goods depots. Gone was traditional wagonload freight. Gone were ageing steam locomotives. Gone was the guard's van from the end of the train (modern automatic brakes had made it unnecessary). In were block trains and containers. In were more efficient working practices and manning levels. BR no longer tried to compete for loads which were better suited for road haulage. Instead, it concentrated on the bulky heavy loads that lorries cannot carry efficiently. BR also looked forward to more profitable freight traffic with Europe via the Channel Tunnel, but that's another story...

Left: **Keeping the lines of communication open, an essential role played by the railways. Hauled by Class 37 No 37021, the 02.42 Liverpool Street-Lowestoft newspaper train is unloaded at Lowestoft in the early hours of 10 September 1983.** *Brian Morrison*

Below: **Freight on the Lea Valley line. Class 31 No 31019 with a down load of scrap passes Class 31 No 31015 with up vans near Coppermill Junction on 3 October 1977.** *Martin Higginson*

1 Coal Traffic

Coal had always been the largest commodity moved by rail. However, as diesel and electric traction began to replace steam, and Natural Gas from the North Sea replaced Town Gas, BR lost a considerable amount of coal traffic. Decisions were made to enable the remaining coal traffic to be handled more efficiently.

There were two big changes which dramatically altered the way coal was moved on BR: Merry-go-round, and the building of Coal Concentration Depots.

The Merry-go-round (MGR) concept was unveiled in 1965, although its full impact was not felt until the 1970s. The idea was to have a continuous supply of coal running from pithead to power station — nonstop like the horses on a fairground merry-go-round.

Special wagons were introduced for this service. These wagons weighed 32 tons, and would remain coupled to the locomotive throughout the operation.

At the pithead, the locomotive would haul the wagons at very low speed under a succession of overhead chutes from which coal was dispensed. The train would then head for the power station. There, the train would move over hoppers beneath the track, and the wagon bottom doors

BARNETBY

Below: **Class 37s Nos 37225/106 thunder through Barnetby with a trainload of bogie hoppers on 1 March 1989.** *Chris Shaw*

Left: **Class 47 No 47314 revs up to pull away from the signal at Barnetby with a loaded MGR coal train on 16 April 1982.** *John E. Oxley*

would open automatically to discharge the coal. Great quantities of coal could be moved quickly this way. By 1980, the MGR concept was arguably the most efficient freight working on BR.

Coal Concentration Depots, introduced in the 1960s, were a major step away from traditional working practices regarding domestic coal. For many years it had been the norm for coal merchants to be based in, or next to, station yards. This enabled them to order relatively small quantities of coal from a colliery (one or two wagons at a time), have it delivered by rail directly to their premises, and then use the stationary wagon as a storage bunker. Not only did this mean a lot of wagonload working over lines not otherwise used for freight, but also a large number of coal wagons would be out of use for long periods of time. By 'concentrating' coal business to key sites, BR was able to eliminate these practices and move coal in bulk. Onward distribution to local coal merchants was made by road, often in BR-owned vehicles.

As the demand for solid fuel for domestic heating (and for industry) declined, another reorganisation was necessary. BR closed many depots in 1984. Coal operations were hived off from Speedlink by 1989 as traffic had dwindled to less than 2.5 million tonnes per annum nationwide. The new operation was christened Network Coal. Services were based around Toton yard, on the London Midland Region.

BURY ST EDMUNDS

Left: **A coal train from Whitemoor arrives at Bury St Edmunds behind 'J17' No 64691 in July 1960.** *John C. Baker*

Focus on Freight

Right: **No 2007, a shunter of what would later become Class 04, works in the coal dock at Bury St Edmunds in 1962.** *John C. Baker*

CAMBRIDGE

Left: **Class 31 No D5634 passes Shepreth Branch Junction signalbox with a coal train from Whitemoor to Broxbourne on 17 May 1969.** *R. Elsdon*

Below: **BR Standard '4MT' No 75037 brings a freight from Bletchley into Cambridge on a cold day in March 1961.** *G. D. King*

Left: **Coal predominates on this mixed freight hauled by Class 37 No 37261 passing Coldham Lane Junction on 4 August 1978.** *Les Bertram*

CRESSWELL COLLIERY

Left: **A loaded MGR train passes Cresswell Colliery on 15 April 1983, behind No 56015.** *Paul D. Shannon*

ELY

Above right: **Class 31 No 31325 crosses the New and Old Bedford Rivers near Manea with a train of coal empties from Ipswich to March on 9 June 1975.** *Stanley Creer*

Right: **As staff check the signals at Ely North Junction, Railfreight Coal sub-Sector-liveried Class 37 No 37308 takes coal empties from Hythe at Colchester and Claydon at Ipswich to March on 14 May 1988.** *Michael J. Collins*

Focus on Freight

FLETTON

In the early 1960s, the Central Electricity Generating Board (CEGB) realised that the coal-fired power stations then being built on the River Trent would create a lot of fly ash, as well as generating considerable amounts of electricity. Although the ash is quite light, it is equivalent to 25% of the weight of the original input coal. To dispose of this ash, the CEGB took over disused brick pits at Fletton, outside Peterborough. The idea was to use fly ash to fill in the pits, then reclaim the land for agricultural use.

The Fletton reclamation site consisted of a large reservoir containing around 500 million gallons of water around which was constructed a 1½-mile MGR-style loop. The facility was capable of receiving up to 10,000 tons of fly ash daily — mostly from Drakelow, West Burton and Ratcliffe-on-Soar power stations.

Above: **A train of fly ash from Ratcliffe, hauled by Class 58 No 58010, at Fletton on 28 January 1984**. *John Rudd*

Below: **Class 47 No 47001 leaves Peterborough with a block train of fly ash on 27 August 1974. Trains** consisted of 48 air-braked Presflo wagons and each train had a capacity of about 1,000 tons of ash. This would be discharged 24 wagons at a time by means of compressed air, mixed with water to form a slurry, and then pumped into settling pits. *Norman E. Preedy*

GAINSBOROUGH CENTRAL

Below: **An MGR coal working from Manton to Immingham rumbles through Gainsborough Central behind '47/0' No 47168 on 1 July 1977.** *Stanley Creer*

HARLOW

Below: **Coal empties for March pass north through Harlow Town behind No 31138 on 28 April 1982.** *Roland Hummerston*

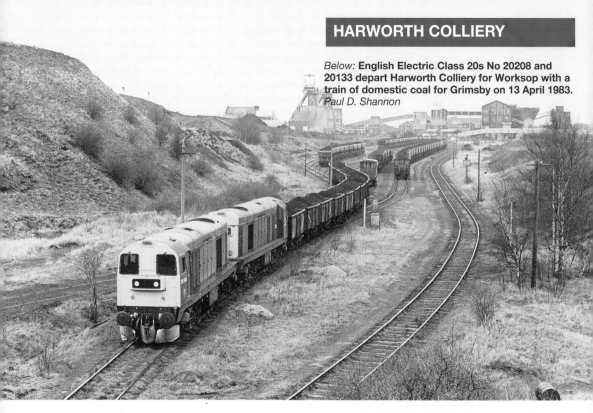

Below: **English Electric Class 20s No 20208 and 20133 depart Harworth Colliery for Worksop with a train of domestic coal for Grimsby on 13 April 1983.** *Paul D. Shannon*

Below: **Although common practice in the USA, it is unusual to see a quadruple-headed train on BR. However, on 22 December 1982 Class 31s Nos 31303 and 31217 required assistance on the Dinnington** line. They are seen here between Brancliffe East Junction and Turnerwood *en route* from Harworth to Worksop with coal hoppers, assisted by **Class 20s Nos 20011 and 20154.** *John Wright*

HATFIELD COLLIERY

Right: **Bearing Railfreight Coal sub-Sector decals on its bodyside, Class 56 No 56015 passes Hatfield Colliery with a loaded MGR for Scunthorpe on 16 February 1989.** *John S. Whiteley*

HIGH MARNHAM POWER STATION

Left: **No 56069 leaves High Marnham Power Station for the run back to Ollerton Colliery with an empty MGR train. Although included in the overall MGR plan, the dead-end layout of the sidings prevented true MGR operation.** *Paul D. Shannon*

Left: **Wearing 'Large Logo' blue livery, Class 56 No 56117 arrives at High Marnham CEGB Sidings with an MGR train on 12 April 1984.** *Paul D. Shannon*

21

Although the dock opened as early as 1912, it was not until the 1960s that coal shipments at Immingham began to take off. This followed the setting up of a working party in 1962 with the objective of raising coal exports beyond the then total of 500,000 tons per year. By 1968 the British Transport Docks Board was expecting exports of coal and coke to reach 3 million tons. MGR shipments to the export dock there reached around 5 million tonnes by 1983, a large proportion of which went to Italy, Denmark and West Germany.

Left: **An Immingham-Aire Valley train of imported coal passes Brocklesby on 8 April 1993 behind Class 56 No 56106. The export of coal through Immingham had slumped by the end of the 1980s, and by this time most of the coal passing through was being imported.** *Michael J. Collins*

IPSWICH

Right: **When Network Coal was set up after the removal of the traffic from Speedlink, Ipswich was designated a coal-receiving depot. Class 37 No 37116 leaves Ipswich Yard with a coal train on 13 July 1976.** *I. P. Cowley*

LETCHWORTH

Left: **The 6M03 03.25 Temple Mills-Toton Network Coal train makes its Letchworth stop on 23 March 1990. The coal was unloaded by a hopper conveyor (just visible above the last of the five wagons). The service was normally the preserve of a Railfreight Coal Class 37, but on this occasion Class 31/4 No 31429 was provided. The Letchworth depot closed in November 1990.** *Paul D. Shannon*

MALTBY COLLIERY

Right: **A number of Class 56s and 58s used on East Midlands and Yorkshire coal duties were named by Railfreight Coal in the late 1980s, with both the collieries and power stations they provided for being commemorated. After its naming ceremony at Maltby Colliery on 22 June 1989, No 56012 prepares to leave with a loaded train.** *Brian Morrison*

OLLERTON COLLIERY

Left: **Class 31 No 31302 arrives at Ollerton colliery with a trip working from Mansfield Concentration Sidings on 15 June 1981.** *Paul D. Shannon*

PETERBOROUGH

Left: **Ex-War Department 2-8-0 No 90223 passes Peterborough North with a coal train in September 1960.** *John C. Baker*

Left: **An up coal train headed by Class O2 2-8-0 No 63956 runs through Peterborough North in April 1961.** *John C. Baker*

Focus on Freight

POOLSBROOK

Right: **Due to emergency repairs to Brookhouse viaduct on 10 August 1981, trains from Markham Main Colliery — which usually ran via Woodhouse to power stations east of Worksop — were diverted up the Clowne line. Usually this line was used for the return of empties only. Here Class 47 No 47372 leads as Class 56 No 56005 pushes from the rear just after leaving Poolsbrook. Upon arrival at Creswell, No 56005 would have been facing the right way and would have continued on to Worksop unaided.** *John Wright*

RETFORD

Left: **'O4' 2-8-0 No 63645 crosses the East Coast main line at Retford with an eastbound train of coke in May 1961.** *John C. Baker*

Left: **Still carrying its pre-TOPS number, but now without the 'D' prefix following the end of main line steam on BR nearly two years before, Class 31 No 5817 passes Retford Low Level with a long train of empty 16-ton end door wagons, (then widely used for coal traffic) on 21 July 1970.** *David Wharton*

SHEFFIELD

Right: **Ex-LMS '8F' 2-8-0 No 48383 approaches Brancliffe East Junction with coal empties from Kirkby on 29 August 1963. Plans were drafted around this time for a new connection between the former Midland Railway and Great Central lines in the Parkgate area. The two routes were only 50yd apart and on nearly the same level. The connection would have allowed Midland line freights to reach Tinsley Yard for locomotive and crew changes.**
A. W. Martin

SIZEWELL

One of the more sensitive cargoes carried by Eastern Region freight trains is irradiated nuclear fuel flasks to and from the region's nuclear power stations and the British Nuclear Fuels reprocessing plant at Sellafield. As the power station at Sizewell is not directly rail-connected, the flasks are taken by road the short distance to the Sizewell siding, and then loaded on to the train.

It was widely accepted that road traffic could not match rail's capabilities for safety and security. Just to emphasise the point, BR staged a mock high speed crash involving a nuclear flask at Old Dalby in 1984. In later years the appearance of nuclear trains was spruced up. Locomotives

were reliveried, and the redundant coal wagons once used as barrier vehicles replaced by purpose-built units.

Below: **Class 37 No 37109 hauls a nuclear waste train from Leiston station on to the Sizewell siding in readiness to receive its cargo on 19 April 1984. Strict safety regulations were applied to this train, and its speed was limited to 45mph. Movement of flasks would take place approximately once every three weeks. The nuclear traffic kept the remainder of the Aldeburgh branch open, from the junction with the East Suffolk line to Leiston. A Radio Electronic Token Block (RETB) equipped Class 37 was hired from the Railfreight Construction sub-Sector for use on this service.** *John A. Day*

SOUTHEND VICTORIA

Right: **The Coal Concentration Depot built at Southend Victoria in 1966/7 was typical of those built across the country as part of the reorganisation under the National Freight Plan. Coal was deposited in different bins by a conveyor moving from the centre of the depot's semi-circular plan, and was then loaded into road vehicles by the conveyor as required through the hopper on the left.** *D. Mackinnon*

SPALDING

Right: **The Great Eastern & Great Northern Joint Line between Spalding and March resounded to a never-ending procession of coal trains from Yorkshire to Whitemoor Yard. 'WD' 2-8-0 No 90484 heads for Whitemoor through Spalding station in September with a loaded train.** *John C. Baker*

WEST BURTON POWER STATION

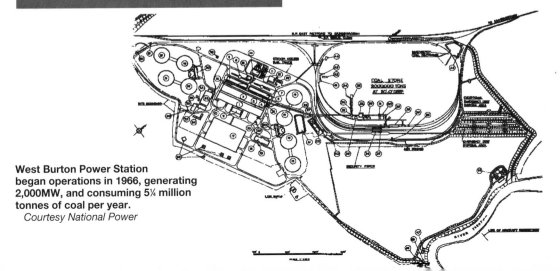

West Burton Power Station began operations in 1966, generating 2,000MW, and consuming 5¼ million tonnes of coal per year.
Courtesy National Power

Left: **Class 56 No 56015 displays its original Rail Blue livery as it leaves West Burton power station with a train of empties on 11 September 1980.** *Les Bertram*

WORKSOP

Right: **An MGR working from Kiveton Park Colliery is hauled through Worksop by No 56113 on its way to Cottam Power Station on 20 September 1983.** *Paul A. Biggs*

Right: **An eastbound loaded MGR train approaches Worksop from Shireoaks on 28 August 1980, hauled by Class 47 No 47213.** John E. Oxley

2 Aggregates

Aggregates by rail were an uncommon sight until the building boom of the 1970s. Before this, the construction industry relied on 'indigenous sources' — sand, gravel and limestone from workings near each construction site.

Due to the nature of the construction business, it was (in most cases) uneconomic to deliver aggregates directly to the work site. Sometimes a temporary railhead could be established near the building site, but this was feasible only on large,

long term projects. Mostly aggregates were transported to the site by road from an established terminal.

Bulk cement and cement products were also carried by rail. The Region's main cement works were at Claydon and Barrington. However, cement and prefabricated materials were also brought in from other regions. Bricks were another construction commodity carried by rail in large quantities.

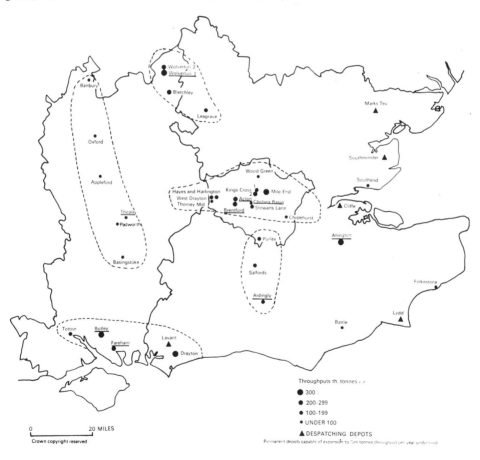

0   20 MILES

Crown copyright reserved

Throughputs th. tonnes

● 300
● 200-299
● 100-199
• UNDER 100
▲ DESPATCHING DEPOTS

Permanent depots capable of expansion to ½m tonnes throughput per year underlined

The diagram shows rail depots for aggregates in the southeast. *Modern Railways*

Below: **Empty roadstone wagons are returned from Redland at Kennett to Mountsorrel behind '25s' Nos 25137 and 25219 on 11 April 1978.**
John C. Baker

Below: **Class 47 No 47276 nears Basildon with a down train of cement tanks on 21 June 1978.**
D. E. Canning

BARHAM

The Tilbury terminal at Barham received limestone from Somerset and granite from Leicestershire. Stone was conveyed in trains of up to 23 51-tonne hopper wagons. Turnaround time at the depot was around 3hr.

Right: **Class 56 No 56064 heads a train from Mountsorrel to Barham on 29 April 1986. This train would have come from Mountsorrel to March as a 'Jumbo' train. There it would be split, with the first portion coming to Barham, the remainder going to the Kennett roadstone terminal.** *John A. Day*

BARKING

Right: **A special train of Blue Circle cement Presflo wagons passes over Barking flyover on 23 June 1960.** *British Rail*

BARRINGTON

Below: **Sentinel No 18 leaves the Rugby Cement works and runs on to the Barrington Light Railway with a trip working to the BR exchange sidings at Foxton on 14 May 1987.** *John C. Baker*

BATTLESBRIDGE

Above: **Class 37 No 37215 hauls a train of sand hoppers from Southminster near Battlesbridge station on 23 August 1978. Sand traffic for Williams Brothers from pits near Southminster began in 1962 with trains of 13 24-ton ironstone wagons each day** to the Mile End depot. This was later expanded to three per day in each direction, plus an additional train on Saturdays. By the early 1970s around 290,000 tons of sand each year were being moved on this route. *G. P. C. Robinson*

BIGGLESWADE

Below: **'31/1' No 31141 arrives with a train from Peterborough on 28 August 1987. An earlier arrival for Plasmor Bricks is already being unloaded.** *Paul D. Shannon*

BISHOP'S STORTFORD

Right: **No 56064 waits as its train of roadstone hoppers is unloaded on 14 July 1989. This former coal depot was converted to a roadstone terminal in the mid-1980s.** *Paul D. Shannon*

BOUGHTON

Right: **In 1983, Butterley Brick obtained permission to build a siding on the site of the former Boughton station goods yard — adjacent to their brickworks near Kirton, Notts. It was opened the following year — on a rather wet day if this photo is anything to go by!** *Courtesy Butterley Brick*

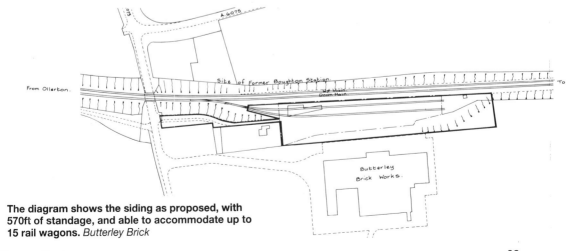

The diagram shows the siding as proposed, with 570ft of standage, and able to accommodate up to 15 rail wagons. *Butterley Brick*

BROOKMANS PARK

Right: **A down special working of cement hoppers from Barking is headed by '9F' No 92188 between Potters Bar and Brookmans Park in June 1960.** *Derek Cross*

CHETTISHAM

Right: **Class 37 No 37087 passes Chettisham with a sand train from Middleton Towers to Doncaster on 15 August 1981.** *John C. Baker*

CLAYDON

Left: **Class 47 No 47276 delivers a freight from Ipswich into the Blue Circle private sidings at Claydon on 23 December 1982. The Christmas time slowdown in the construction industry is well reflected here.** *John C. Baker*

Focus on Freight

GRAYS

Below: **A trainload of building materials from Grays nears West Thurrock behind Drewry 0-6-0DM No 11131.** *Frank Church*

HARLOW

In 1980, the former BR goods depot site at Harlow Mill was taken over by Foster Yeoman for use as a stone terminal. It handled approximately 200,000 tonnes of aggregates per year.

Below: **Class 59 No 59005 shunts in the sidings at Harlow Mill on 14 July 1989.** *Paul D. Shannon*

KENNETT

Below: **Class 47 No 47064 passes Kennett with a stone train for the Redland siding on 25 November 1982. The ferry van on the right is from Italy and has brought a load of basketware for Newmarket. It was unloaded at Kennett despite the overgrown state of the yard.** *John C. Baker*

Below: **The 10.05 block train of private-owner wagons reverses into the Redland siding at Kennett on 7 March 1979.** *John C. Baker*

KETTON CEMENT WORKS

Below: **Class 47 No 47576 nears Wood Croft crossing with a train to Castle Bromwich on 3 January 1984. Because trains cannot reverse at Ketton, they travel the 14 miles to Peterborough in the wrong direction, before heading west towards Leicester.** *John C. Baker*

KING'S CROSS

Below: **Class 08 shunter No 08670 shunts HTV hopper wagons from a Fen Drayton sand train on 28 October 1987.** *Paul D. Shannon*

Right: **Wagons from Ketton are shunted into the Castle Cement sidings at King's Cross by No 08709 later the same day. The Marcon gravel terminal can be seen to the right.**
Paul D. Shannon

KING'S LYNN

A significant traffic through King's Lynn was sand for Rockware glass from nearby Middleton Towers. This service began on 2 October 1968.

Left: **No 31322 moves to a halt at Middleton Towers with a sand train for King's Lynn on 4 February 1981.** *C. E. Dann*

Left: **Class 31 No 31313 enters King's Lynn yard with a sand train on 15 April 1980.**
J. C. Hillmer

Focus on Freight

Below: **Standard '9F' No 92040 approaches Knebworth with cement empties on 25 May 1963.** *D. Percival*

Below: **Class 31 No 31325 nears Magdalen Road station with a trainload of sand from King's Lynn to Whitemoor on 11 June 1975.** *Stanley Creer*

MARCH

Below: **A sand train from Middleton Towers leaves March South Yard for Doncaster on 9 February 1980. Plenty of coal traffic is still in evidence, and the goods shed is still standing, though abandoned.** *John C. Baker*

MARKS TEY

Below: **Class 47 No 47014 prepares to leave Marks Tey with a sand train on 11 August 1987. Sand from the Brush Aggregates sandpits at Bellhouse Farm, in the valley of the Roman River, was moved by** road the two miles or so to Marks Tey goods depot. There it was loaded into former ironstone hoppers by mechanical shovel and transported to the Mile End terminal — a journey of about 1hr 40min. This service began on 19 November 1969 with two trains of 24 wagons (600 tons) per day, and would continue on to become one of the last vacuum-braked freights on the **Eastern Region.** *Michael J. Collins*

Below: **A sand train formed of 'RH Roadstone' bogie hoppers leaves Marks Tey behind '31s' Nos 31240 and 31180 on 1 September 1989.** *Michael J. Collins*

MILE END

The stone terminal at Mile End was originally a coal depot. The coal drops were adapted as bins for loading aggregates by mechanical shovel.

Below: **Class 31s Nos 31272 & 31268 stand at Mile End with a sand train from Marks Tey on 8 September 1987. As freight services to the Mile End terminal had to be fitted in between suburban and long distance passenger trains on a busy main line, drops had to be strictly controlled and timed.** *Brian Morrison*

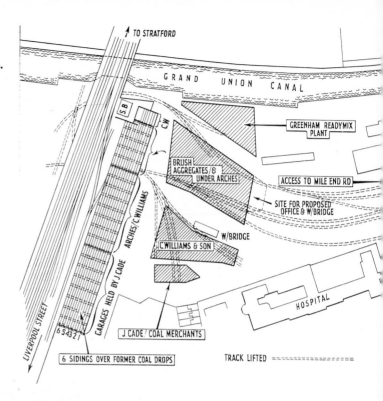

Right: **As the diagram shows, a number of merchants used the yard including Williams Brothers and Brush Aggregates. Greenham, a Taylor Woodrow subsidiary, operated the adjacent ready-mixed concrete plant.**

TO STRATFORD

GRAND UNION CANAL

S.B

C.W

GREENHAM READYMIX PLANT

BRUSH AGGREGATES / 8 UNDER ARCHES

ACCESS TO MILE END RD

ARCHES / C.WILLIAMS

SITE FOR PROPOSED OFFICE & W/BRIDGE

W/BRIDGE

C.WILLIAMS & SON

GARAGES HELD BY J CADE

LIVERPOOL STREET

6 5 4 3 2 1

HOSPITAL

J. CADE / COAL MERCHANTS

6 SIDINGS OVER FORMER COAL DROPS

TRACK LIFTED ====================

PETERBOROUGH

Below: **Gresley 'V2' No 60845 passes Peterborough North with an up cement train in July 1961.**
John C. Baker

Peterborough had much brick traffic until the 1960s. By 1967, however, this had dwindled to five block loads per week from Fletton to Gateshead, Stockton or Laisterdyke. During the 1970s all remaining links with brickyards were severed and all bricks were transported by road.

Peterborough also had considerable cement traffic.

Right: **No 64171 leaves Peterborough with a trip working to Fletton in September 1960.**
John C. Baker

Right: **Grimy, dirty, workaday freight — in the pouring rain. 'J6' 0-6-0 No 64177 passes Peterborough North with a trip working from the Fletton brickworks to New England Yard in September 1960.**
John C. Baker

PURFLEET

The Foster Yeoman terminal at Purfleet was opened early in 1980 on the site of the former BP oil terminal. All stone was brought from Somerset in combined trains of up to 50 wagons (5,100 tonnes) which were split at Acton into trains of up to 30 wagons to Purfleet and 20 to Harlow Mill.

The wagons used were former British Steel PTA wagons and, from 1988, box wagons built by Orenstein & Koppel. They were shovel and grab unloaded, taking approximately 10min per wagon of 75 tonnes.

Right: **'56s' Nos 56048 and 56040 *Oystermouth* begin the return journey to Somerset with their empty Foster Yeoman hoppers, on the morning of 17 April 1984.** *Brian Morrison*

REEPHAM

Left: **A train of concrete girders passes Reepham on the freight-only line from Lenwade to Wroxham behind No 31176 on 21 July 1976.** *Ray King*

RETFORD

Left: **No 90601 waits for a clear signal at Retford station in May 1961. The train is mostly of building materials.** *John C. Baker*

SPALDING

Left: **A trainload of sand for Rockware Glass comes off the line from March at Spalding on its way to Yorkshire behind No 31309 on 12 May 1979.** *Les Bertram*

STEVENAGE

Left: **A down cement train is headed past the 'ha'penny bridge' north of Stevenage by '47' D1796 on 24 October 1970.** *P. R. Foster*

Lower left: **Ballast trains passing between Stevenage and Hitchin on 14 June 1970. The locomotives are Class 31 Nos D5587 and D5628.** *P. R. Foster*

STRATFORD

Below: **Class 31 No 31263 joins the Great Eastern main line at Stratford with a train of bogie bolster wagons from Temple Mills on 26 May 1977.** *Kevin Lane*

SWAVESEY

Right: **A sand train from Fen Drayton crosses the level crossing at Swavesey on 29 July 1983. Sand from the Fen Drayton quarry was sent to Allington, Wood Green and King's Cross.**
Roland Hummerston

THREE HORSE SHOES

Right: **Class 37 No 37193 passes Three Horse Shoes signalbox with a block train from Middleton Towers to Monk Bretton on 21 July 1983.**
John C. Baker

WHITWELL QUARRY

Right: **Class 56 No 56058 waits as its train is loaded with limestone at Whitwell on 17 August 1990. The train was bound for Witton.**
Paul D. Shannon

Focus on Freight

3 Manufactured Goods

The railways formed an essential link between factory and market. In some areas, such as the automotive industry for example, movement by road would have lowered the goods' value. At one time or another just about everything went by rail. From fibres to firewood, beer to butter, coins to cars... The General Railway Classification Book gave an exhaustive list. Official figures for 1962 show that merchandise was the second biggest freight revenue earner for British Railways, with more than 72,000 tons being moved nationwide in a 40-week period. But things were already on a downward spiral. Many manufacturers found road more convenient, especially on the routes which had direct motorway competition. A byzantine system of tariffs did not help the railway's position.

Speedlink would later embrace much of this traffic. Other traffic, which could be moved more efficiently by road, was discarded.

A vast amount of manufactured goods were sent by the wagonload, and there were some important changes in wagonload operations before the advent of Speedlink.

First of all, a wide variety of cargoes required a wide variety of wagons. Some wagons were

BROOKMANS PARK

Below: **An up van train hauled by Brush 4 No D1518 heads south of Brookmans Park on 31 May 1963.** *Brian Stephenson*

privately owned, but most belonged to BR. Some wagons had vacuum brakes, some had no continuous brake at all, and thus relied on the braking power of the locomotive at the front of the train and the guard's van at the rear. Whilst the differences between privately-owned and BR-owned wagons did not cause many problems, the variations of braking systems did. When diesel power began to take over from steam, it soon became apparent that diesel-hauled services required greater braking power as speeds were higher. By the mid-1960s, there were seven different classes of freight traffic all based on speed and braking characteristics. This made diagramming of trains difficult and caused problems in organising crews. Clearly the situation could not go on, and after trials had taken place, it was decided to reduce the number of classes from seven to two: Class 4 and Class 7. Class 4 trains were vacuum-braked express freights and block trains. Class 7 trains were unbraked, slower trains. Class 7 'Star' services were diesel-hauled throughout and, therefore, slightly faster as they did not need to stop and take on water. In the 1970s, air-braked services would be added to the equation.

CAMBRIDGE

Right: **Cambridge was an important centre for freight, as seen by the packed sidings here on 3 April 1970. '03' No 2009 shunts a short cut of wagons, including two containers mounted on Conflat wagons and one placed in an open truck.** *J. H. Cooper-Smith*

Below: **Leaving Cambridge on the Newmarket line, the experimental Roadrailer train is seen on a trial run from Goodmayes Yard on 17 May 1962. This innovative method of transport consisted of specially adapted lorry trailers (with both road and rail wheels and braking systems), enabling the trunk part of the journey to be made by rail. Sadly this mode of shipment did not take on. The coach next to D5699 is a dynamometer car.** *BR*

DAGENHAM

The massive Ford Motor Company works dominates the area around Dagenham. Since the early 1960s, when Ford opened its plant at Halewood on Merseyside, rail transport between the two sites has been a crucial part of the company's manufacturing process. Block trains would move components between the two factories and virtually formed part of the production line. Finished cars would also leave Dagenham by rail, either for export or distribution around the country.

Above: **Empty 'Cartic' articulated wagon sets stand in the foreground at Dagenham Dock on 9 February 1978 as a '302' unit hustles by from Fenchurch Street. Behind the passenger train are Carflats loaded with Transits and Cartics loaded with Ford Cortinas and Escorts.** *John Glover*

Below: **Former BR Class 04 No D2267 was sold out of service in 1970 to become No 1 in the fleet used on the Ford internal railway system at Dagenham. Just months after it had returned to its birthplace for a full overhaul, the Swindon-built locomotive shunts Ford internal user wagons at the exchange sidings with BR on 9 February 1978.** *John Glover*

ELMSWELL

Above: **A special working of Leyland cars from Dorridge to Parkeston Quay passes through Elmswell behind No 37283 on 8 March 1982.** *John C. Baker*

FINSBURY PARK

Below: **A mixed freight bound for King's Cross Goods Yard approaches Finsbury Park in October 1961 behind Class 24 No D5052.** *Brian Haresnape*

GAS FACTORY JUNCTION

Right: **A mixed goods for Bow crosses Gas Factory Junction, behind No D8014, then only 18 months old.** *Frank Church*

GRANTHAM

Below: **'A3' Pacific No 60063** *Isinglass* **thunders through the cutting between Grantham and Great Ponton with an up freight on 13 April 1963. By 1980 there would be virtually no daytime freight on the former East Coast main line south of Grantham.** *T. Boustead*

HIGHAM

Above: **A van train from Felixstowe passes the closed station at Higham, between Bury St Edmunds and Newmarket, in the charge of No 5668 on 7 September 1970. The headcode 6M30 suggests that the eventual destination of the train was the West Midlands (King's Norton), but it did not always run through beyond Whitemoor, as was the case on this occasion.** *G. R. Mortimer*

HITCHIN

Below: **Class 47 No D1102 passes Hitchin with an up working of empty Cartic 4 wagons and (at the rear of the train), some loaded Carflats. Under the National Freight Plan of the mid-1960s, Hitchin was included in the Temple Mills zone. This was because the majority of wagonload traffic from Hitchin went south, not north. It was felt that Temple Mills was more suited to handle outward wagonload services.** *J. H. Cooper-Smith*

KING'S LYNN

Above: **English Electric '37' No 37283 crosses the Fens with the 15.08 freight from King's Lynn to Whitemoor on 29 May 1986. The first three wagons are from Campbell's Soups. The firm of Campbell was a long-time rail user, with products leaving its King's Lynn private siding for Scotland. When the Campbell King's Lynn factory opened in 1958, much of its output went by rail. Rail traffic then ceased from Campbell, but in 1975 began again, the company hiring 15 PVB side-curtain vans. By 1983 a fifth of the output of the Campbell factory was moved by Speedlink. Once arriving at Whitemoor, the three vans of soup would be fed into the Parkeston-Mossend service for the journey north.** *John C. Baker*

LEA BRIDGE

Centre left: **Fowler '4F' No 44297 passes Lea Bridge with an up mixed freight from Temple Mills on 12 November 1960.** *L. Sandler*

MARCH

Below left: **A Harwich-Whitemoor fitted freight passes March East Junction in November 1968.** *R. Elsdon*

Above: **Class 31/4 No 31418 nears Manningtree with a train from the Rowntree plant at Chelmsford to York, on 23 December 1985.** *John C. Baker*

Below: **Class 37 No 37054 approaches Lancaster's Crossing, near Stowmarket, with the 19.23 Speedlink service from Mossend to Parkeston on 11 May 1985.** *John C. Baker*

SANDY

Below: **An up freight is accelerated through Sandy by Class 9F No 92035 in April 1963.** *C. F. Burton*

Below: **Ex-War Department 2-8-0 No 90223 passes Sandy with a down freight in August 1960.**
John C. Baker

ST NEOTS

Below: **Brand new Brush 4 No D1505 heads (appropriately!) a Class 4 freight near St Neots on a winter's day in the early 1960s.** *Bishop Eric Treacy*

The railway was (and is) the main carrier of raw materials for iron and steel production, as well as many of the finished products. Coal, oil and limestone used in the steel and iron smelting process were also transported by rail — mainly in private owner wagons. Scrap metal was another important traffic transported to steelworks by rail.

The late 1980s saw an increase in rail-borne steel traffic. On the Eastern Region there were significant inland ore flows from Immingham to Scunthorpe, and long distance flows of fluxes and scrap to Sheffield and the northeast.

Finished steel was imported into ports like King's Lynn and transported in VTG wagons with sliding hoods. Terminals were built at Barking, Bow Creek, and Immingham to enable steel coils to be handled under cover. By 1987 Railfreight had captured 20% of the steel import market.

Below: **Former War Department 2-8-0 No 90683 enters Whitemoor, from the Peterborough line, with a train of steel waste in September 1960.**
John C. Baker

BARNETBY

Left: **Iron ore was moved by MGR as well as coal. Class 60 No 60019 approaches Nab's Bridge, Barnetby, with an MGR train from Immingham to Scunthorpe on 30 October 1990.** *Alan Morgan*

CHESTERFIELD

Left: **Ex-LMS '8F' 2-8-0 No 48153 hauls a northbound iron ore train at Chesterfield in May 1965.** *D. Booth*

DONCASTER

Below: **A trainload of steel pipe sections awaits the road at Doncaster behind 'B16' No 61435 in April 1961.** *John C. Baker*

ELMSWELL

Above: **A special working of scrap metal destined for export to Japan passes Elmswell on its way to Lowestoft on 17 February 1979 behind No 37036.** *John C. Baker*

LEA BRIDGE

Below: **Class 31 No 31263 hauls an up mixed freight train (mainly of coke and steel) through Lea ridge on 3 October 1977. The Lea Bridge Parcels Depot can be seen to the right of the picture.** *Martin Higginson*

NEWMARKET

Right: **A train of export steel from Scunthorpe to Felixstowe nears Newmarket on 9 March 1984.** *Michael J. Collins*

ROTHERHAM

Left: **Class 20s Nos 20127 & 20017 double-head a train of steel coil for Sheffield through the old Rotherham station on 21 September 1976.** *Brian Morrison*

Focus on Freight

SCUNTHORPE

Right: **An empty train of 21 bogie tipper wagons is hauled at speed towards Immingham, from Scunthorpe, by two Class 37s on a summer day in 1974. The completion of Scunthorpe's Anchor project in 1972 brought about an upsurge in freight traffic to and from Immingham.** *Colin Boocock*

SHEFFIELD

Right: **Class 31 No 31301 takes the Sheffield avoiding line over the Tinsley-Aldwarke Junction freight-only line with a train of ore tippers on 31 October 1977.** *C. R. Davis*

SILVERTOWN

Left: **A somewhat frustrated railman pushes shut the gate at T. W. Ward behind a trip working from Temple Mills to Silvertown on 15 April 1986 — scarcely surprising as the train was some 3hr late! The abandoned second track on the level crossing and remnants of a loading gauge give mute testimony to the fact that rail-borne scrap traffic had decreased over the years. The locomotive is No 31238.** *Paul D. Shannon*

SNAILWELL

Above: **Class 37 No 37885 heads a train of scrap from Snailwell to Whitemoor on 14 June 1990. Section 8 grants in the 1980s had enabled new wagons to be used on this route.** *John C. Baker*

WARE

Right: **Class 31 No 31128 heads from Ware to Hertford with a train of tube wagons on 14 September 1978.** *John Glover*

WISBECH

Left: **Wagons of steel coil, which originated in Wales, are shunted in the Metal Box sidings at Wisbech by Class 08 No 08418 on 29 April 1986.** *John C. Baker*

Perhaps the area of greatest decline on the Eastern Region was that of agricultural traffic. In its heyday, this traffic was quite heavy. Fruit, vegetables, seed potatoes, sugar beet, flowers, livestock and fish were all — at one time — carried by rail.

Many wholesale markets were rail-connected. At Sheffield, a new line was built in 1962 to allow the market recently built by Sheffield Corporation to be rail-served.

Around 75% of UK fish tonnage was landed at east coast ports. Rail-borne fish traffic was heavy, and at its peak more than 200 wagonloads were received at King's Cross Goods Yard each night. This traffic diminished rapidly after 1964 as the BR Board felt it was a loss-maker. Average payloads per train went down to around 32 tons which was barely enough to cover the operating costs. By 1966 there was only one fish train from Grimsby to London each day, and it only contained (on average) 15 wagons. This service ended in 1967.

Livestock traffic too was lost to road transport. It was considered costly and labour-intensive, so BR was not too sorry to see it go.

The cut-back of rural lines in Cambridgeshire and the rest of East Anglia forced many farmers to abandon rail transport all together. Lincolnshire potato farmers also deserted rail for road transport.

Sugar beet and the other materials used in the refining of sugar continued to be rail-borne for a while, and this traffic was heavy during the sugar beet harvesting season or 'campaign'. This lasted from September to January and necessitated a lot of wagon movement from country stations. At its

Below: **A pick-up freight arrives at Bury St Edmunds from Cambridge behind 'J17' No 65582 in February 1962. The train is mostly formed of open wagons loaded with sugar beet, although there are also three Calor gas wagons from private sidings at Saxham & Risby.** *John C. Baker*

height, sugar traffic resulted in more than 82,000 wagon movements per year.

The wagons used for beet traffic were coal wagons. After being emptied at a coal merchants, they were pressed into service before being returned to the colliery. When raw sugar was dispatched for refining, 16-ton mineral wagons were used. These were specially caulked and fitted with sheet supporter bars.

Most sugar beet traffic was over short distances. It was estimated that 60% of the beet crop was harvested within 20 miles of the nearest sugar factory, and 90% within 30 miles. Some beet was grown in the south of England and transported to East Anglia by rail.

At one time thirteen sugar beet factories were located within the Eastern Region. The British Sugar Corporation's factory at Ipswich (for example) would process around 75,000 tonnes of beet each year. Output could be as much as 870 tonnes per day — much of it going by rail, but this had ended for the most part by the mid-1970s.

Grain traffic, however, proved for some years an exception to the rule of decline in agricultural produce. Bulk movements of malt and grain — particularly to Scottish distilleries — grew from the mid 1960s onwards.

In 1980, Grainflow was set up as a joint venture between Railfreight and Traffic Services Ltd (TSL). It hired privately-owned wagons — mainly Polybulks — from other companies on five-year contracts.

Polybulk wagons were designed and built in France. They consisted of three hoppers in a covered vessel, were built of steel, had a capacity of 58 tonnes and weighed 80 tonnes gross. Polybulk wagons were already widely used on the Continent, and TSL arranged for 30 to be transferred to the UK for the launch of Grainflow.

Many grants were made under Section 8 of the Railways Act (1974) to improve grain handling facilities. At Eccles Road, on the Ely-Norwich line, a new branch line was needed to cope with the increased traffic!

Left: **North British Type 2 No D6122 shunts at Thurston with the early morning pick-up goods from Ipswich to Bury St Edmunds on a cold January day in 1960. The train comprises grain wagons and 16-ton opens, the latter probably to be used to carry sugar beet.** *John C. Baker*

ANCASTER

The Distillers Company used to transport grain from Ancaster to maltings at Burghead in Morayshire.

Left: **In 1965, Distillers ordered 115 bulk grain wagons for use on this, and other, services. Tare weight was just under 13 tons and capacity was 22 tons. The hopper body was of welded steel. They were capable of being worked at speeds of up to 60mph. Distillers was quick to utilise the advertising potential of these wagons. They were painted in a distinctive blue livery, and hoardings advertising the company's many brands of whisky were carried on the sides.** *United Distillers*

BIGGLESWADE

Right: **A portable grain elevator is seen in use at Biggleswade on 25 August 1961. This device enabled grain to be loaded straight from a lorry into a bulk grain van, thereby cutting out the need for the grain to be sacked and loaded into a closed van by hand.** *British Rail*

BISHOPSGATE GOODS

Bishopsgate Goods was completely destroyed by fire on the night of Saturday 5 December 1964. The fire was one of the biggest the capital had seen since World War 2, with 67 appliances and 300 firemen in attendance. It was never rebuilt.

Below: **Like many inner city goods terminals, Bishopsgate Goods was originally a passenger station. It was converted to freight use when Liverpool Street station was opened. The depot dealt mainly with continental traffic via Harwich. It handled freight from Russia, Iran, Turkey and nearly every country in Europe — except those which used the Southern Region channel ports. It also handled perishables and sundries from the Lea Valley. Here we get a superb view as an RCTS special departs in September 1953.** *R. E. Vincent*

Above: **Class 2MT No 46465 leaves the down sidings with a trainload of sugar beet for the British Sugar Corporation factory further down the line towards** Thurston, in October 1960. The factory produced granulated and castor sugar — as well as animal feeds. *John C. Baker*

DISS

Below: **Brand new Scottish Malt Distillers wagons wait on a siding at Diss on 27 April 1983. These were worked in circuit to the Muir of Ord. Note Diss's other traffic — UKF fertilizer and coal.** *John C. Baker*

DOWNHAM MARKET

Right: **This siding at Downham Market was typical of the many built with Section 8 grants, and served the flour mill in the background.** *Michael J. Collins*

ELY

Right: **A trainload of imported timber passes through Ely** *en route* **from King's Lynn to March behind D8204 in August 1961. Like Cambridge, railway geography made Ely an important East Anglian railway centre with much through traffic.** *John C. Baker*

GIDEA PARK

Left: **Class 31 No 31238 hauls an up milk tank train near Gidea Park on 7 September 1981.** *Alex Dasi-Sutton*

Eastern Region

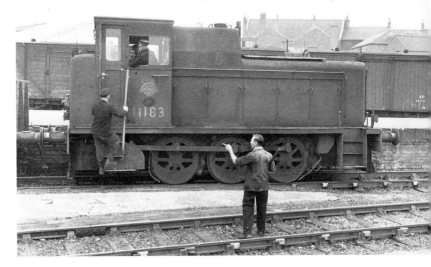

Left: **Wagons from the Banks grain siding at Kennett are collected for the 11.45 Bury St Edmunds to Whitemoor freight on 21 March 1979. The ferry van had brought in binding additive from Europe to mix with second class barley to make animal feeds.**
John C. Baker

Below left: **Class 31 No 31206 passes Kentford *en route* from Ipswich to Whitemoor with a train of agricultural machinery and fertilizers, on 25 May 1978.**
John C. Baker

KING'S LYNN

Above right: **Andrew Barclay No 11183 shunts at King's Lynn in April 1961.** *John C. Baker*

Finished products were also shipped out by rail. These included various types of granulated and liquid sugar, molasses and animal feeds. Speedlink distribution was ideal for this type of cargo.

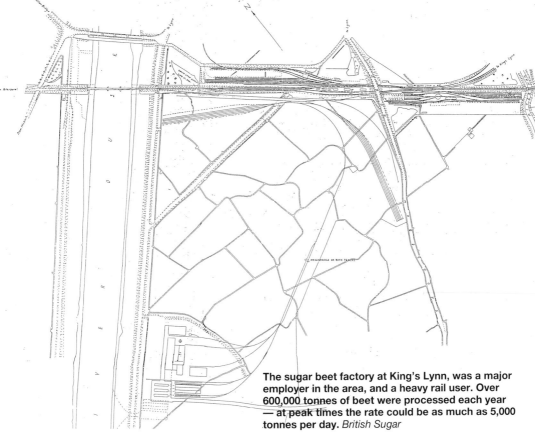

The sugar beet factory at King's Lynn, was a major employer in the area, and a heavy rail user. Over 600,000 tonnes of beet were processed each year — at peak times the rate could be as much as 5,000 tonnes per day. *British Sugar*

MARCH

Below: **Grainflow Polybulks predominate on this train from Duxford into Whitemoor, passing March behind No 31109 on 11 April 1984.** *John Rudd*

Above: **Class 31 No 31146 stands in the sidings at Newark Northgate on 12 January 1981. Note the loading gauge above the locomotive — this is typical of simple but effective apparatus to be found at many goods yards and sidings.**
C. J. Tuffs

Below: **As evening falls, Lincoln-based Class 08 shunter No 08418 crosses the Trent Navigation with a short van train from Newark Castle to Northgate on 4 March 1976. Newark's two stations — Castle and Northgate — both had goods facilities.**
Rev Graham B. Wise

A rare, but none the less important, commodity carried by Eastern Region trains was racehorses, which were regularly carried by rail to Newmarket until 1966. Horses were unloaded in the station goods yard and walked the two miles to the racecourse stables at the Links. The horses probably enjoyed this exercise after a long journey — although it's doubtful their lads did!

Railway loose boxes were very comfortable for the horse, with leather padding and plenty of straw on the floor. In addition to forming special trains, horse boxes were often coupled to the end of express passenger trains.

Section 8 grants were particularly valuable in areas such as Newmarket. The nature of much of the agricultural traffic in the area (grain, for example) required specialised loading equipment that could not otherwise have been afforded.

Below: **Class B1 4-6-0 No 61287 approaches Newmarket with a Horse Race Special from Redcar and Doncaster.** *Ian Allan Library*

Left: **Class 37 No 37084 prepares to leave a siding at Newmarket, for Cambridge, with a train of grain Polybulks on 25 May 1983.** *John C. Baker*

NORWICH

As a rural area, almost completely devoid of heavy industry, the traffic around Norwich was predominantly wagonload. In the reorganisations of the 1960s, however, much of this traffic was considered unprofitable and was discontinued.

Right: **Class 31 No 31122 waits at signals outside Norwich with a freight from Fakenham, as a DMU passes on 25 June 1975.** *Brian Morrison*

PETERBOROUGH

Right: **Class 47 No 47527 passes the sidings of the Peterborough sugar factory with a special from King's Cross to the Nene Valley Railway on 3 December 1983. The large amount of sugar beet to the right of this picture was typical of the sight to be seen near sugar beet factories at the height of the 'campaign'. Raw sugar from Peterborough was transported to refineries at Cupar in Scotland, or Silvertown in east London, in block loads. Some beet pulp went to the Midlands, whilst raw beet was transported to Kidderminster.** *John Rudd*

Left: **Class 31 No 31182 passes Soham with a train formed of bulk grain vans and hoppers, on 4 May 1979. This train was carrying malt from Mistley to Scotland.** *John C. Baker*

SPALDING

Left: **A down cattle train passes through behind 'O2' No 63981. The transport of cattle, sheep and pigs was a trade BR discontinued in the late 1960s.**
John C. Baker

Below left: **The London International Freight Terminal (LIFT) opened on 4 July 1967 and was built on a 35-acre site formerly used for carriage sidings. Its construction was hastened by lack of facilities following the Bishopsgate fire.** *Aerofilms 91/COL/78*

Built at a cost of £1.5 million, LIFT was specifically designed to deal with continental import/export traffic. It took all such traffic previously handled at Stratford Market, Lea Bridge, Mile End and Chobham Farm depots.

Right: **The diagram shows how the central area of LIFT looked when opened. The road entrance in Temple Mills Lane was well connected to the existing and planned road system of east London, and the whole complex was conveniently situated next to the Stratford Container Terminal.**

The capacity of the holding sidings was 95 ferry wagons, the reception sidings held three trains. Perishables such as fruit and vegetables were given priority and cleared and unloaded as quickly as possible.
Modern Railways

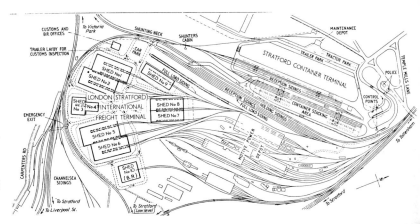

Right: **Inside one of the sheds, around 1970.** *Courtesy Railfreight Distribution*

Below: **Type 1 No D8243 passes LIFT and Stratford Freightliner terminal with a mixed freight on 29 October 1968.**
J. H. Cooper-Smith

THURSTON

Below: **A train of sugar beet pulp nuts, bound for St Blazey, from Ipswich, passes Thurston behind '31/0' No 31005 on 29 December 1977.** *John C. Baker*

WYMONDHAM

Below: **Class 31 No 31109 comes off the North Elmham branch with grain Polybulks from North Elmham to Burton upon Trent on 17 April 1984.** *Paul D. Shannon*

WHISTLE W

Practical Freightliner development got under way in 1962. A standard 8ft by 8ft square cross-section was adopted. Standard lengths were set at: 10ft (7½ tons rated load), 20ft (15 tons), and 27ft (20 tons). The 27ft length was dictated by the road vehicle length limitations then in force in the UK. When this was changed to allow 30ft containers, the 27ft length was phased out. Later the development of a 9ft high container would cause problems for BR, as it was too tall to fit under the UK standard loading gauge. The containers themselves were of a light alloy construction.

The container concept was not new. As long ago as 1926, the four British main line companies introduced a door-to-door container service. BR had been running small 5-ton containers for many years prior to the 'container revolution' of the mid-1960s.

The ability to lift what would be several small loads — sacks or boxes for example — in one movement was very attractive to hauliers. Customers benefited from reduced damage in transit, less pilferage, and all weather reliability. Shock-free transit for delicate objects — like TV

Below: **A prototype Freightliner train makes a test run from the King's Cross (York Way) terminal on 25 May 1965.** *Courtesy Railfreight Distribution*

sets and other breakables — appealed to insurance companies, which offered lower rates for goods sent via Freightliner than for goods sent by road or conventional rail movement.

It was realised quite early on that it would be uneconomic to provide adequate transfer equipment at every station goods yard. It was, therefore, decided to concentrate container traffic on a few principal centres and use road vehicles for collection and delivery. Dedicated Freightliner Terminals (FLTs) were built at key cities and ports.

The first Freightliner trains ran from King's Cross Goods Yard in 1966. Services from this terminal were phased out in the 1970s when operations were concentrated on Stratford and Willesden. Between 1964 and 1969 more than £25 million was invested in Freightliner.

Freightliners Ltd was established in 1968 as part of the National Freight Corporation. The Transport Bill of 1978 gave BR 100% ownership.

In 1983, Freightliners Ltd joined the Stock Euro Group for greater flexibility with exports to the EC.

Freightliner flat cars were 60ft long and had a rigid draw bar coupling system. The were permanently coupled in rakes of five. Each Freightliner wagon was expected to travel around 70,000 miles per year.

A new system of tariffs was developed for Freightliners. This was based on the size of the container and the route. The direction of the train and the type of cargo did not matter. This was a complete departure from conventional practice. An incentive discount scheme was also offered.

Below: **English Electric Type 4 diesel (later Class 40) No D279 passes St Neots with a down freight, around 1960. Note the small 5-ton containers on the first three wagons behind the locomotive.** *Eric Treacy*

Focus on Freight

Above: **Class 47 No 47372 heads south away from Cambridge with a Freightliner service on 4 August 1978.** *Les Bertram*

Below: **Special cranes were built specifically to handle containers. This one shown at an unknown FLT is typical of many built in the 1960s and 70s.** *British Rail*

CHELMSFORD

Right: **Class 47 No 47052 approaches Chelmsford with a Felixstowe-bound Freightliner train from Stratford on 1 March 1984.** *Michael J. Collins*

CLAYDON

Right: **Class 47 No 47289 approaches the level crossing at Claydon with a special Freightliner service from Felixstowe to Leeds and Stockton on 16 November 1985.** *John C. Baker*

FELIXSTOWE FREIGHTLINER TERMINALS

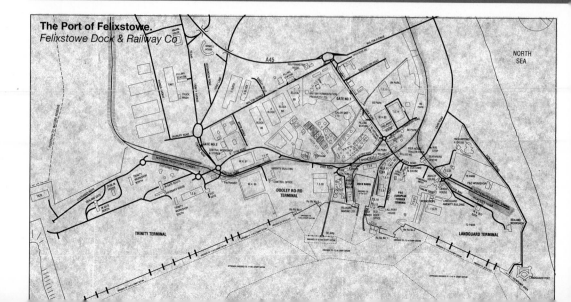

Two Freightliner terminals were constructed at this burgeoning Suffolk port: the Southern, opened in 1972, serves the Landguard container terminal; the Northern, opened in 1983, serves the Dooley and Walton terminals. A third container terminal, Trinity, opened in 1986.

By 1985 Felixstowe's two Freightliner terminals were handling around 130 flat cars each way per day. On an average day, 30 to 40 cars were consigned to destinations other than those specified on the train plan. Such adaptability was vital to the deep sea container trade.

Below: **Class 37 Nos 37154 and 37209 stand in the Northern Freightliner terminal, ready to depart with a train for Coatbridge on 10 July 1989.** *Paul D. Shannon*

HAUGHLEY JUNCTION

During 1981, sawdust was transported from Great Yarmouth to Coatbridge by Freightliner. The material was loaded into specially adapted containers and sent down to Ipswich in a special train. This train would then connect with the overnight Freightliner service from Felixstowe to Coatbridge.

Right: **Class 31 No 31314 passes Haughley Junction with the 12.16 'sawduster' on 29 May 1981.** *John C. Baker*

IPSWICH

Left: **A Freightliner train hauled by Class 47 No 47357 passes Ipswich *en route* from Stratford to Felixstowe on 1 August 1980. By 1989, Freightliner traffic was going directly from Ipswich to Birmingham, Garston, Stratford and Willesden.** *I. P. Cowley*

LEVINGTON

Left: **A Cambridge-Felixstowe Freightliner passes Levington on 21 March 1987.** *Michael J. Collins*

MAIDEN LANE

Maiden Lane was at the forefront of the container revolution. The first revenue-earning Freightliner train on the Eastern Region left Maiden Lane at 20.05 on 15 November 1965, bound for Glasgow. The train consisted of 13 wagons carrying 39 containers. Only three, however, contained a commercial load — the rest had lengths of old rail for ballast.

Left: **The Mk 2 Drott Crane transfers a 27ft covered container at Maiden Lane in 1965. Facilities at Maiden Lane were basic and were soon outgrown. After closure its cranes were used at Stratford for a while. The site later became a housing estate.**
Courtesy Railfreight Distribution

Right and Below: **Brush Type 4 (later Class 47) No D1697 hauls a prototype Freightliner train out of Maiden Lane in May 1965. Note the caboose on the leading wagon. Following complaints from BR staff, this type of accommodation for the guard was withdrawn before Freightliners entered active service.**
Courtesy Railfreight Distribution

PURFLEET

Left:
Class 47 No 1762 hauls a Willesden-Grays Freightliner at Purfleet on 2 March 1973. *Brian Morrison*

RIPPLE LANE FLT

The Freightliner terminal at Ripple Lane opened in 1972. In 1974 it was remodelled as a centre for company trains.

Above: **The Freightliner terminal's crane can clearly be seen behind the activity of East Yard, as Class 47 No 47193 passes with a tank train on 18 April 1984. Ripple Lane FLT had trains to and from Manchester (Barton Dock Road), Southampton, Tilbury and many other destinations.** *Paul D. Shannon*

Left: **Class 37 No 37122 awaits departure from Ripple Lane with an up tank train, as a Freightliner train waits to be unloaded on 19 December 1981. Ripple Lane FLT was intended to be the London terminus for Southampton maritime traffic.** *Brian Morrison*

STRATFORD FLT

Right: **Services from Stratford ran to Edinburgh, Stockton, Hull, Newcastle, Leeds, Southampton, Cardiff, Bristol, Trafford Park, Ipswich Griffin Wharf, Felixstowe, Harwich Parkeston Quay, Tilbury, Willesden, Holyhead, Coatbridge, Cleveland, Swindon and the private freightliner terminal operated by Dagenham Storage.** *Courtesy Railfreight Distribution*

Right: **A Freightliner train pulls away from Stratford in the late 1980s. In 1987 Freightliner joined forces with Tank Container Services to provide a door-to-door service for tank owners in the UK & European import/export markets. Under the scheme — which was named 'Mastertank' — depots at Felixstowe and Stratford were set up to provide services for bulk liquid and powder traffics. Each depot was equipped with 38-tonne tractor units fitted with compressors and operated in conjunction with step frame trailers.** *Courtesy Railfreight Distribution*

Right: **Stratford FLT on 14 May 1968. A Freightliner service between Stratford and Paris La Chapelle-Annexe via the Dover-Dunkirk train-ferry began on 22 April 1968. Sadly, it lasted only a year — its tariff was not competitive enough. Later import services were introduced to Tilbury, Felixstowe and Harwich. Running time to Harwich Parkeston Quay was about 2hr.** *Courtesy Railfreight*

Eastern Region

TILBURY FLT

The container terminal at Tilbury was commissioned in 1968 and opened in 1970. It was sited on former exchange sidings between the Port of London Authority (PLA) and BR, and consisted of a four-lane roadway with two sidings spanned by a 30-ton six-wheel crane. The site had no facilities for storage, which was unusual. Tilbury had services to and from Barking, Barton Dock Road, Birmingham, Coatbridge, Felixstowe (south), Garston, Leeds, Swindon, Trafford Park and Willesden.

Below: **Class 37 No 37358 *P & O Containers* hauls a trip working of containers from Tilbury Docks to the FLT on 11 September 1988. It was unusual for a locomotive of this type to be working in the docks complex. The usual motive power here would be a Class 08 shunter from Stratford Depot.**
Brian Morrison

Left: **Following the official naming ceremony, staff and management of the Tilbury FLT pose with the presentation nameplate from Class 37 No 37059 *Port of Tilbury*. Freightliners Ltd took over the running of the terminal from the Port of London Authority in the early 1980s.** *Brian Morrison*

Focus on Freight

7 Speedlink

During the 1970s, BR continued to improve on the changes made in the 1960s. With more efficient working, and new air-braked wagons replacing older vacuum-braked ones, Railfreight launched a new concept in wagonload freight: Speedlink.

Officially launched on 13 September 1977, Speedlink was a network of daily services using fast, high capacity, air-braked wagons and linked main industrial and market areas. It used TOPS to keep track of wagons, and trains ran to a given timetable — just like passenger trains. The network was designed around private sidings, rather than station goods yards — most of which were subsequently closed. Section 8 of the Railways Act (1974) and its grants for private siding facilities attracted many customers who had not previously used rail transport.

Below: **Class 37 No 37259 hauls a Speedlink train past Needham Market on 13 May 1986.** *John C. Baker*

By 1981 the network had expanded to cover 11 trunk routes. *Modern Railways*

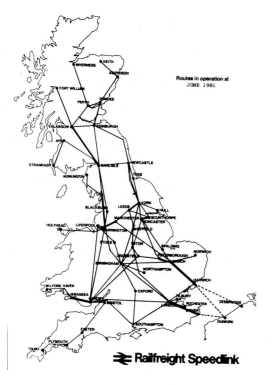

Routes in operation at JUNE 1981

≷ Railfreight Speedlink

Speedlink Development Plan

SPEEDLINK ROUTE & YARD NETWORK

Route		No of trains per day, 1982*	
		Out	Home
1	+++++++++	3	3
2	++++++++	3	3
3	‒ ‒ ‒ ‒ ‒	7	6
4	――――	6	6
5	++++	9	9
6	―――	9	8
7	+++++	2	2
8	········	7	8
9	+++++	3	3
10	+++++	2	2
11	～～～	2	2
		53	**52**

○ Nodal yards on trunk network
□ Subsidiary yards

This map shows the trunk routes only.
* Some trains will run over part of the route only.

Speedlink was initially a success. Around 25% of traffic carried was new to rail. This was largely the result of an intensive and highly successful marketing campaign.

By 1982, the busiest Speedlink route was the Harwich-northeast England-Scotland service. Other Eastern Region routes were: Harwich or Whitemoor to Paisley, Mossend, Warrington, Tees, Widnes and Oxford. Most carried continental traffic. Household coal, still a wagonload commodity, was integrated into the Speedlink network in 1983, and in May 1984 conventional wagonload freight movements were abolished. All individual wagon movements were integrated into the Speedlink system.

Freightliner and Speedlink were merged by BR in 1988 to form a single group: Railfreight Distribution. In 1990, Railfreight Distribution made the shock announcement that Speedlink was to close. It had become too uneconomic to operate. As volume declined, the unit costs per wagon towards infrastructure items like locomotives and marshalling yards increased. The more expensive things became, the less inclined companies were to use the system, and the more money BR was forced to pump in to keep the network running. It was a vicious circle. By the end Speedlink made up only 2% of Railfreight business. It was estimated that the closure of Speedlink put an additional 300,000 lorry movements on to the roads.

ELY

Below: **The advent of Speedlink arrested the decline of rail traffic at Ely. The Papworth terminal opened in 1982, providing a combination of goods services and private involvement in rail. The terminal handled bulk stone from UK quarries, tinned fruit, engine components, wood and paper products, as well as imported powder products for the pharmaceutical industry. All this was in addition to the extra grain traffic that Speedlink helped to generate. Following its official naming ceremony on 23 September 1987, Class 37 No 37068** *Grainflow* **leaves Ely for March with four Polybulks.** *John A. Day*

LAKENHEATH

Above: **A Speedlink freight from Norwich to Whitemoor nears Lakenheath behind Class 31 No 31406 on 29 August 1985.** *John C. Baker*

MARCH

Below: **A Harwich Parkeston Quay-Warrington Arpley Speedlink service arrives at March on 16 July in the charge of No 47011.** *John Rudd*

MISTLEY

Above: **VDA and VAB vans form a special munitions train hauled by Class 31 No 31128, seen at Mistley on the Harwich branch in July 1984. Traffic for the** **Government, Royal Ordnance and Ministry of Defence was carried by Speedlink on long term contract.** *Michael J. Collins*

Focus on Freight

Above: **Class 47 No 47281 heads north at Peterborough with a Speedlink train of ferry vans on 19 June 1984.** *W. A. Sharman*

Below: **As New England Yard was a primary staging area, Peterborough saw many Speedlink services in the 1980s. Class 47 No 47296 leaves Peterborough with a Speedlink from Ipswich to Paisley Underwood on the evening of 2 September 1982.** *John Rudd*

THURSTON

Below: **The 16.38 from Harwich Parkeston Quay to Doncaster passes Thurston behind No 47097 on 11 June 1986.** *John C. Baker*

WISBECH

Above: **Pedigree Petfoods at Wisbech demonstrated one of the most efficient uses of Speedlink — two-way traffic. Pallets of canned petfood were brought by Speedlink from Paisley, and empty cans (brought by road from Grantham) made the return journey. The old goods yard at Wisbech — once considered for closure — was** adapted for forklift operations at a very modest cost.

No 47309 prepares to leave with a train to Whitemoor on 15 July 1987. In addition to petfoods, household coal and seasonal seed potatoes were also brought in from Scotland to Wisbech by Speedlink. *Brian Morrison*

Focus on Freight

Just as the nation's demand for coal decreased over the years, the demand for oil rose dramatically. Much of this was rail-carried, especially the output from North Thamesside refineries. By 1963, it was accepted that road transport could not match the bulk carrying capabilities and quick turnaround of equipment that rail had to offer; nevertheless, BR was not satisfied with its share of the expanding oil market and launched a vigorous campaign to capture more. This was the beginning of the block train era, and oil was one of the first success stories.

Between 1962 and 1972, domestic oil consumption in the UK rose by nearly 90%. However, after 1973 the tonnage carried by rail, and the amount consumed, decreased rapidly. This was due mainly to massive price increases. The increased use of pipelines for oil movement also took away traffic from the railways.

BR's performance in chemicals traffic, on the other hand, was harder to assess in terms of market share. A diversity of materials: gas, powder, liquids and solids, were all categorised as chemicals.

Below: **Class 40 No 40162 passes the disused Thurston signalbox with a tank train from Whitemoor to Harwich Parkeston Quay on 25 May 1977.** *John D. Mann*

Most chemicals were transported in private-owner wagons. In 1977 it was estimated that, nationwide, fewer than 2,000 wagons used for chemical traffic belonged to BR compared to around 3,000 privately owned. Wagons for chemical traffic fell into three broad categories: tanks (for both liquids and gases), vans (for bagged fertilizer etc) and hoppers (for bulk solids such as potash). Some of these wagons (cryogenic tanks, for example) were very expensive, but as their life could be up to six times longer than equivalent road vehicles, they were seen as a good investment — particularly as the cost of new lorries and spares rose by nearly 170% between 1972 and 1977! Section 8 grants encouraged many chemical companies to change to rail transport.

Above: **An early block train of petrol tankers approaches the signals controlling the entrance to Little Ilford yard. The refineries on the north bank of the Thames were heavy rail users, and it is likely that this train originated there.**
Frank Church

Left: **At the beginning of the block train era, Standard '9F' No 92183 passes Thames Haven Junction with a special tank train of Fisons chemicals for Immingham.** *P.R. Gillet*

BARKING

Below: **Class 47 No 47012 leaves Barking with a train of petrol tankers on 15 May 1980.**
Les Bertram

BLACK BANK

Below: **Class 37 No 37044 passes Third Drove Crossing, near Black Bank, with empty tanks from Peterborough to Ripple Lane on 31 July 1984.**
John C. Baker

BURY ST EDMUNDS

Above: **Class 40 No 40084 passes through Bury St Edmunds with a train, formed mostly of tank wagons, from Mossend to Harwich Parkeston Quay on 12 July 1979. Note the changed layout compared to earlier photographs.** *John C. Baker*

CAMBRIDGE

Left: **A tank train headed by Class 47 No 47180, approaches Cambridge on 1 March 1979. Two years earlier, in 1977, Esso petroleum expanded and revamped its Redline Oil Services bulk distribution depot at Cambridge. The new facilities included a 330ft siding from the Cambridge-Ely line, capable of accommodating up to 11 rail tank wagons. During peak times, two 300-ton trains could be received.** *John M. Capes*

Focus on Freight

Below: **Class 45 No 45130 passes Cambridge in April 1984 with a tank train to the nearby Ciba Geigy works at Duxford.** *I. J. Hodson*

GAINSBOROUGH

Below: **Class 47 No 47223 pulls away from Gainsborough Lea Road with a trainload of TEA tanks for Immingham on 9 February 1989.** *Brian Morrison*

There were many oil wells in the Gainsborough area. This oil was piped to holding tanks in Lea Road Goods Yard, and then loaded on to tankers. Oil from Gainsborough would be dispatched to refineries at Llandarcy in South Wales, Grangemouth in Scotland and the Immingham refineries on Humberside. Traffic usually amounted to two or three trainloads per week.

GRAYS (WEST THURROCK)

Above: **Class 37 No 6824 hauls a down tanker train at Grays on 6 September 1973.**
Brian Morrison

Left: **A block train of VIP tank wagons carrying naphtha, leaves West Thurrock for the Tipton (Staffs) gas works on 28 September 1966.** *British Rail*

Focus on Freight

IMMINGHAM

The refineries and oil traffic from Immingham saw rapid expansion in the 1960s. Shell, Regent Oil (later Texaco), Petrofina, Total and Continental (Jet) all opened or expanded their Humberside facilities during this time.

Below: **The industrial complex skyline can be seen on the horizon as Class 37 No 37114 leaves the port with oil tankers for Leeds on 30 June 1977.** *Stanley Creer*

Below: **A block train of Total oil tanks approaches Ulceby on the freight-only Immingham branch later the same day.** *Stanley Creer*

IPSWICH

Left: **Class 31 No 31138 waits in the centre road at Ipswich with an empty tanker train from Norwich to Ripple Lane on 30 December 1977.**
John C. Baker

KENNETT

Left: **A UKF bogie van for bagged fertilizer sits on a siding at Kennett on 12 July 1983.**
John C. Baker

LINCOLN

Left: **Class 31 Nos 31278 & 31117 pass through Lincoln with bogie tanks on 26 August 1986. Trains from Total's Lindsey refinery would run via Lincoln to the Langley terminal on the Western Region near Slough.**
Mick Alderman

Above: **Class 47 No 47336 passes Lincoln Central with empty bogie tanks on 11 February 1987.** *Mark Scott*

NORTH WALSHAM

Below: **An unusual cargo carried by rail is North Sea Gas condensate from the Shell terminal at North Walsham. In this photograph, Class 47 No 47367 prepares to leave with a tanker train for Parkeston on 27 December 1990.** *Michael J. Collins*

STEVENAGE

Above: **Class 37 No 6741 passes Stevenage with an up oil train on 22 March 1972.** *Dr R. Elsdon*

Below: **Class 47 No 1872 passes Langley Sidings with an up oil train on 31 January 1970. The HEA coal wagon often used as a barrier vehicle next to the locomotive on such workings is just visible at the rear of the train!** *J. H. Cooper-Smith*

Above: **Class 37 No 37709 leaves the Shell refinery at Thames Haven with a trip working for Temple Mills on 10 February 1989. In the early 1980s Shell invested £14 million in its Coryton refinery. This enabled around 30 trainloads per week to be dispatched.** *Michael J. Collins*

Right: **Having arrived with a trip working from Ripple Lane, Class 37/8 No 37893 leaves the Mobil exchange sidings at Thames Haven on 2 August 1990. At the time the Mobil refinery was dispatching, on average, 40 trainloads per week.** *Paul D. Shannon*

WHITTLESEY

Right: **A forklift unloads pallets of fertilizer at Whittlesey on 1 May 1974.** *British Rail*

WHITTLESFORD

Above: **Class 37 No 37097 deposits tanks in the Myhills siding, Whittlesford, on 1 June 1981.** *Brian Morrison*

9 Ports & Docks

It was deemed logical, even in the earliest days of railways, to link railways to docks and ports. Even when the railways had lost ground to road haulage, the most efficient movement of bulk solids and liquids, or heavy cargoes like steel and building materials, was directly from a ship on to a train at the quayside.

As a trading nation, Britain's economy depended on a sustained flow of exports and imports. Membership of the EC concentrated much of this traffic on the east coast ports. As the rail gauge was the same in Britain as in many continental countries, the advent of roll-on/roll-off vessels meant that cargoes could make their entire journey — sometimes across several countries — without having to be unloaded. Special wagons, called ferry vans, were used for this type of traffic.

Some multinational companies divided the process of manufacturing their products between several factories in different countries (this was particularly true of the car industry). The most

efficient way of shipping components and incomplete products was by rail and sea.

The 'container revolution' of the 1960s changed for ever the way most deep sea cargo was handled. Many ports — notably Felixstowe, Harwich and Tilbury were reconstructed to cope with this traffic.

In some cases the deep sea container trade had no option but to use rail for transport to and from ports. Government restrictions on lorry sizes and axle weights ensured that rail was used for part of the journey. Before the building of the M11 and M25, the roads in East Anglia were not suited for this type of cargo anyway. Rail was deemed the most efficient way of connecting the manufacturing centres and market-places of the main cities with the east coast ports.

Below: **The MV** *Steel Shuttle* **is unloaded at Alexandra Dock, King's Lynn, in January 1986.** *J. C. Barrett*

BOSTON

Below: **Class 08 shunter No 08386 positions Polybulks for loading at Boston on 31 July 1984. The grain silo at Boston Docks was owned by Lingrain — a local farmers' co-operative. Grain from here was forwarded to Glasgow and Leith for processing. Imported steel was also forwarded by rail. The docks were owned and operated by the local council.** *Paul D. Shannon*

FELIXSTOWE DOCKS

Originally opened in the 1870s, the Port of Felixstowe did not become a major port until after World War 2. Although rail-connected from the beginning, direct connections were severed in the 1950s. From then until 1970, when a new curve was opened, the only way trains could reach the docks was by reversing down the link from Felixstowe Town Goods Yard. The following year, the Felixstowe Dock & Railway Company purchased nearly 60 acres of ex-MoD land to expand the port. Its first Freightliner terminal opened in 1972.

In 1986, a new connection was built to link the port with British Rail. This involved a new junction at Trimley station on the Ipswich line and provided direct access to the North Freightliner Terminal. Scheduled traffic began on 16 February 1987. The diagram shows the port layout that year, with the new line to the left.

Left: **In 1972, 2.8 million tons of cargo passed through the port, comprising nearly 106,000 container movements. Container traffic would soon exceed that of any other port in the UK. Apart from a few commodities such as steel coil or paper, container traffic was the mainstay of railway operations here.** *Courtesy Railfreight Distribution*

Focus on Freight

Right: **Class 37 No 6819 leaves Felixstowe Docks with a Freightliner train to Harwich on 17 April 1969. The dock railways were run by the Felixstowe Dock & Railway Co, although the trains were operated by British Rail.** *H. N. James*

Right: **A typical busy scene at Felixstowe in 1987.** *Courtesy Railfreight Distribution*

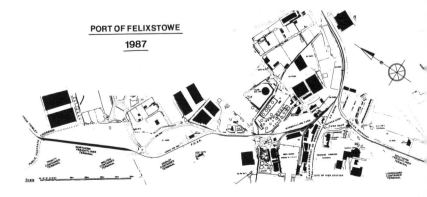

Right: **The Port of Felixstowe in 1987.** *Modern Railways*

PORT OF FELIXSTOWE

1987

HARWICH PARKESTON QUAY

'A showpiece which ... people will come from all over the world to see' predicted Stanley Raymond, Chairman of the British Railways Board, in May 1966 at the beginning of the reconstruction programme that would make Harwich a major modern port. The redevelopment cost £9 million, and was laid out with rail-borne container traffic in mind, as the diagram shows.

The mainstay of rail services was the Harwich to Zeebrugge container service. This began operation on 18 March 1968. Later sailings to Rotterdam and Dunkirk were added. Roll-on/roll-off services were also provided from the start.

Until the 1980s the shipment of vehicle components and complete cars from Ford factories in Britain and Germany was a considerable import/export flow through Harwich.

The port was successful from day one, with approximately 30,000 containers carried in 1968. By 1973 this figure had increased to more than 100,000. In 1986, however, Freightliners Ltd moved its operation from Harwich to Felixstowe. This was due to its change from Sealink to the West German company Comar on the Zeebrugge route. The switch came after the loss of 65% of Ford traffic due to its adoption of the 'super cube' container, which was too large to fit on the railways in the UK.

Below: **Railway and dock facilities at Harwich (Parkeston Quay).** *Modern Railways*

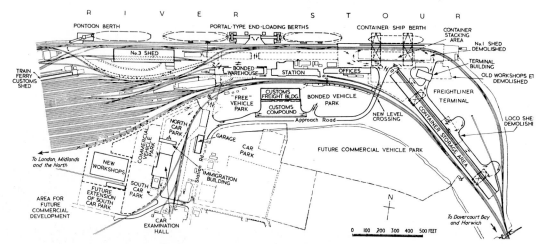

Left: **Class 47 No 47172 nears Bradfield on the Harwich branch, heading a train of containers and ferry wagons for Halewood, on the afternoon of 17 April 1979. Initially the port was served by four Freightliner trains daily; setting up direct links with Stratford, Birmingham, Cardiff, Liverpool and Manchester. Later additional services were provided to Leeds, Glasgow, Holyhead, Bristol, Southampton Millbrook, Willesden and Coatbridge.** *Michael J. Collins*

Right: **A trainload of ferry wagons approaches Parkeston Quay on 4 September 1981. The Sealink train-ferry between Harwich and Zeebrugge was discontinued on New Year's Eve 1986.** *Brian Morrison*

IPSWICH DOCKS

Right: **The relatively narrow quayside is highlighted in this photograph taken on 27 February 1975. By 1983, Ipswich was rated sixth largest on the nationwide table of container ports.** *R. A. King*

Right: **Class 03 shunter No 03179 shunts at Ipswich Docks on 1 December 1976. '03s' were the heaviest locomotives allowed over the bridges which gave access to the docks. A year later, the Ipswich Port Authority was given a Section 8 grant of £120,000 towards the cost of improving facilities at the West Bank ferry terminal.** *I. P. Cowley*

Eastern Region

The partnership between the railways and the port of King's Lynn lasted more than 125 years. The port railways lost ground to road transport during the 1960s and 1970s, but things began to pick up in the 1980s. For a short while in the early 1980s a significant flow of Freightliner wagons used the system for container work diverted from Southampton as a result of industrial relations difficulties. In 1985 timber shipments resumed after a 20-year absence. In 1987 a bulk flow was attracted, with mineral haul Polybulk wagons being used to convey petroleum coke for Rugby Cement's Barrington works. This peaked at around 100,000 tonnes per year.

Left: **The MV *Candourity* discharges bulk urea into Tiger wagons provided by Mineral Haul Ltd at Alexandra Dock on 19 December 1986. Up to 40,000 tonnes of bulk urea per year were transported in Polybulk wagons to Ciba Geigy at Duxford.** *John C. Barrett*

Left: **Around 1986, Associated British Ports — which runs the docks — hired four VTG covered wagons for steel imports, supplemented by up to five BR open wagons. Traffic by rail to the West Midlands steel terminals peaked at about 18,000 tonnes a year using Speedlink services. This ended in 1990.** *John C. Barrett/ABP King's Lynn*

Left: **A train of steel coils is moved off the dock branch into King's Lynn station yard on 6 August 1985. British Rail provided the dock railway with motive power in the form of a Class 08 shunter, along with a driver and shunting staff. The engine was stabled in King's Lynn station freight yard.** *John C. Barrett*

Rail services to the London and St Katharine's Docks were quite poor. This was due largely to their being built prior to the railway age. They were reached via a branch from London Docks Junction on the Fenchurch Street line. This led to East Smithfield Depot and the wool warehouse. This line was unique in London's Docklands, in so much as it was operated by BR Eastern Region rather than the Port of London Authority.

LONDON DOCKS

Below: **East Smithfield Depot closed on 1 January 1966, but the building was still standing and clearly visible in this aerial photograph of St Katharine's Dock taken on 16 October 1968. The Commercial Road Depot is also visible to the north of the Fenchurch Street line.** *Aerofilms SV961*

LOWESTOFT

Right: **A container is loaded on to a ship at Lowestoft in the 1980s. Rail-borne fish traffic from Lowestoft ended in 1972. By that time, only two vans of fish offal — destined for pet food — were dispatched each night.**
Courtesy Railfreight Distribution

ROYAL DOCKS

The Royal Docks (Royal Victoria, Royal Albert and King George V Docks) were rail-served from the beginning. Lines were operated by BR and the Port of London Authority (PLA). Between them the Royal Docks provided about half of the deep sea berths in London, and handled ships of up to 30,000 tons.

Centre left: **The centre of rail activity in the docks was the Royal Victoria Exchange Sidings (shown here in 1961). These comprised three groups: Outwards — 10 tracks capable of accommodating 369 wagons; Reception — 11 tracks able to accommodate 464 wagons; and Marshalling — 10 tracks with a total capacity of 367 wagons. Trains were brought into the reception sidings by BR, where a PLA loco took them over. The main commodities handled were meat, fruit, coal, grain, flower and frozen foodstuffs.**
Museum of London, PLA Collection

Lower left: **A PLA 0-6-0 shunter waits at the Royal Victoria Dock quayside in 1961. Rail services to the Royal Docks were withdrawn by BR and the PLA on 1 May 1970.** *Museum of London, PLA Collection*

STRATFORD

Right: **English Electric Type 1
Bo-Bo (later Class 20) No D8018
passes Stratford Low Level with
a mixed freight on 3 June 1961.
This train was probably heading
for the Royal Docks.**
J. C. Haydon

TILBURY DOCKS

When container operations started at Tilbury, it
was decided to lift all dockyard rail track. Any
non-container merchandise was to be handled by
National Carriers lorries. An exception was made
for lines to the grain terminal. This terminal was,
at the time of its construction, one of the most
advanced in the world, and capable of discharging
bulk carriers at the rate of 2,000 tonnes per hour.

In September 1978, the Northfleet Hope
Container Terminal came into operation. This
terminal had the largest refrigerated container
stack in the world, and could maintain
temperatures between -250°C and +13°C. It was
used for imported meat and dairy products from
Australia and New Zealand.

Right: **Tilbury in the 1980s.**
Port of Tilbury

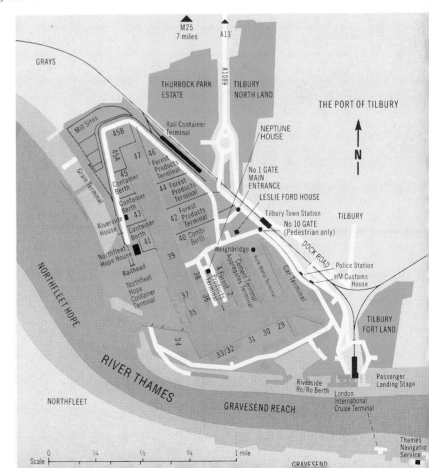

Eastern Region

Left: **An onboard crane unloads a container from a ship at Tilbury in the 1970s. When the container berth at Tilbury was commissioned in 1968, it was expected to deal with one ship and 1,000 containers each week.** *Courtesy Railfreight Distribution*

WEST INDIA DOCKS

Left: **The West India Docks were rail-served from quite early on, although their facilities were not as extensive as those at the Royal Docks further downstream. A rare moment of quiet is shown in this night picture of the exchange sidings. As with the Royal Docks, all rail services were withdrawn on 1 May 1970.** *Museum of London, PLA Collection*

YARMOUTH

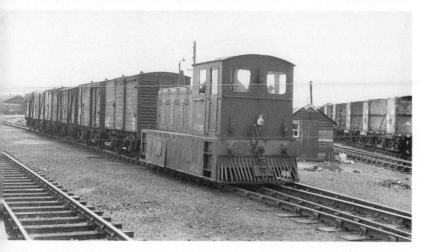

Left: **Class 04 shunter No D2212 shunts freight for the quayside at Yarmouth (Vauxhall) in August 1960. The autumn herring season was the busiest time of the year here, with many fast fish trains being dispatched each day.** *John C. Baker*

Focus on Freight

10 Marshalling Yards

The yards were the hubs of the freight network. As wagonload and Speedlink trains did not go directly from A to B, marshalling yards were vital to freight operations.

Yards did not just deal with marshalling trains. Most had offices and crewing facilities, and some had adjacent freight unloading facilities or Freightliner terminals.

There was an established yard hierarchy: Main Yards — like Whitemoor and Temple Mills were supported by Subsidiary Sidings and Local Sorting Sidings. 'Trip workings' would move wagons between them.

The National Freight Plan of 1965 reorganised the Main Yards into Primary and Secondary classifications. Primary Yards, King's Cross for example, were capable of making up complete trains for at least two other yards. Secondary Yards, like Whitemoor, would make up trains for as many destinations as possible. Both would handle local incoming and outgoing traffic.

With the rundown of wagonload freight in the late 1970s, another reorganisation was called for. The previous hierarchy was, therefore, adapted to meet new demands. The network was reorganised around Network Yards. These would be supported by Section Sidings and Local Terminals. There were also Terminal Complexes — these were usually rail-served industrial estates which needed the shunting requirements of a large terminal.

The advent of Speedlink did away with this hierarchy altogether. It was based around Trunk Yards and a small number of Terminal Yards. These were linked by feeder services. Delivery of wagons to private sidings was made from each of these yards.

Below: **Ipswich Yard on 14 February 1977, as Class 40 No 40167 passes with a train from Harwich Parkeston Quay to Mossend.** *I. P. Cowley*

DONCASTER

The massive changes which took place with the decline of wagonload freight, and the advent of Speedlink and Freightliner services are illustrated well at Doncaster, where freight used to make up 90% of railway business.

By the 1980s, many changes had taken place. Doncaster's Belmont Yard was completely remodelled for Speedlink.

Below: **BR Standard Class 9F 2-10-0 No 92020 leaves Doncaster with a van train on 30 September 1967.** *J. H. Cooper-Smith*

Left: **A Speedlink train leaves Belmont Yard for Mossend on 23 July 1986.** *K. Hacker*

Focus on Freight

FERME PARK YARD

Above: **A pair of Class 31s, Nos 31125 and 31170, take a special parcels train past Ferme Park on 5 March 1988.** *Michael J. Collins*

Right: **Class 47 No D1773 awaits crew relief at Ferme Park with a down '100-ton' petrol train on 28 November 1970.** *P. R. Foster*

GOODMAYES YARD

Left: **A fine panorama of Goodmayes Yard can be seen behind Brush Type 2 (later Class 31) No D5593 as it leaves with a mixed goods for East Anglia on the morning of 13 March 1962.** *M. Edwards*

Left: **Class 11 No 12107 shunts wagons over the hump at Goodmayes on 13 March 1962.** *M. Edwards*

Left: **A train of ferry wagons from Harwich passes Goodmayes on 11 September 1969, behind Class 37 No 6743. Goodmayes Yard closed when Temple Mills was rebuilt.** *J. H. Cooper-Smith*

GRIMSBY WEST MARSH YARD

Left: **The depressed state of the freight scene at Grimsby is well reflected in this picture of West Marsh Yard taken on 12 April 1983. The yard is practically devoid of any activity — except for some steel coils and a few tanks. Many of the lines have already been lifted. The locomotives are Class 31 No 31195 and Class 08 No 08743.** *Paul D. Shannon*

Focus on Freight

IPSWICH YARD

Right: **Class 04 No D2241 shunts in the yard at Ipswich on 3 September 1969. The Griffin Wharf spur and lower goods yard were later used for Freightliner traffic until the opening of a purpose-built Freightliner terminal by the Ipswich Port Authority, on the site of the former Cliffe Quay power station in 1977.**
J. H. Cooper-Smith

KING'S CROSS

King's Cross was designated a Primary Yard under the National Freight Train Plan of 1965. Because it was not well laid out to deal with incoming traffic, its zone extended only as far as Potters Bar. It was nominated a Primary Yard almost entirely because of its originating traffic.

Below: **A fitted freight heads north from King's Cross behind '9F' No 92187 on 27 April 1963.**
Gerald T. Robinson

NEW ENGLAND YARD (PETERBOROUGH)

The 1960s saw a dramatic reduction in the scale of freight train operations in the Peterborough area. The National Freight Train Plan required New England Yard to handle 950 wagons per week, compared to 2,200 five years before.

Under the National Freight Train Plan, New England was classified as a Primary Yard.

Right: **Class 37 No 37066 comes off its train with coal for Eastfield Yard, New England on 21 April 1983. The remains of the former West Yard can be seen in the distance.** *W. A. Sharman*

Below right: **A heavy cement train travelling southwards passes New England on 13 February 1974 behind Class 47 No 1806. The shunter is '08' No 3542.** *Phillip D. Hawkins*

NORWICH THORPE YARD

Below: **A train of petroleum empties for Ripple Lane pulls out of Thorpe Yard on 17 April 1984. At the height of Speedlink services the yard handled 120 wagons per week.**
Paul D. Shannon

RIPPLE LANE YARD

Below: **A typically busy scene at Ripple Lane on 26 November 1982. Class 47 No 47378 backs on to oil tanks from Coryton, while No 47377 waits to leave with an up oil train from Thames Haven. Ripple Lane** yards were built to serve the oil refineries, chemical works, cement works and container port on the north bank of the Thames. Most traffic was bound for regions other than the Eastern. *Brian Morrison*

Left: **An HEA wagon built for MGR work provides the barrier on an oil train leaving Ripple Lane on 26 August 1969 in the charge of Class 47 No 1888.** *J. H. Cooper-Smith*

Left: **With the yard in the background, Class 37 No 6825 passes Ripple Lane with a train of Presflo wagons on 2 August 1969.** *J. H. Cooper-Smith*

Left: **Class 47 No 1676 *Vulcan* enters Ripple Lane with an oil train on 26 August 1969.** *J. H. Cooper-Smith*

Focus on Freight

SCUNTHORPE (TRENT & NEW YARDS)

In 1971, it was decided to switch the functions of Scunthorpe's two yards. Trent Yard, with a capacity of only 400 wagons per day, would sort inward empties, while New Yard (next to Scunthorpe station) became the site for a new outward terminal yard. The intended capacity of the New Yard was 1,100 wagons per day.

Right: **A variety of finished steel products can be seen in Scunthorpe New Yard in September 1980.** *Les Bertram*

TEMPLE MILLS YARD

Remodelled in the 1950s, Temple Mills was Britain's second automated marshalling yard, and was equipped with the then latest in electronically-controlled retarders.

The main traffics under Speedlink/Freightliner operations were to and from the Haven ports, Tilbury, Stratford, Dagenham, Felixstowe and Harwich Parkeston Quay.

Below: **An up freight arrives at Temple Mills yard on 14 June 1967, hauled by Brush 2 No D5637. Temple Mills was the Eastern Region's principal yard in the London area and handled traffic to and from other regions, City freight depots and the London Docks. Its capacity was set at 4,500 wagons per day over the hump and was designated a Primary Yard.** *P. H. Groom*

Above: **Temple Mills on 15 May 1980. The main traffic was to and from Whitemoor, bringing in traffic from the North and Midlands. Trains served the yard by means of a double track main line from Stratford to Coppermill Junction, leading from the Cambridge main line.**
P. H. Groom

Left: **Class 31 No 31133 approaches Temple Mills with a trainload of scrap on 19 June 1979. The passage of time is quite noticeable here, when compared with the scene in 1967. The decline of wagonload freight operations meant that by the late 1970s another remodelling was necessary. The yard was rationalised for Speedlink in 1982.** *P. H. Groom*

Focus on Freight

TINSLEY YARD

Right: **No 13003 pushes a train over the hump at Tinsley on 20 September 1976. Tinsley's traffic included fuel oil, pig iron, iron ore, steel scrap, coal and coke and finished steel products.** *Brian Morrison*

Below: **Tinsley Yard on 1 September 1980, with Class 13 'master & slave' combination No 13001 in the foreground. Destinations for outward traffic included Lincoln, New England, Hull, Birkenhead, Liverpool Brunswick, Doncaster, Whitemoor, King's Cross, Ferme Park and Worksop.** *Paul D. Shannon*

Tinsley Yard was designed to handle traffic to and from the Sheffield industrial region. More than 70% of its traffic was of local origin or destination; 80% of that was private siding traffic.

The main function of the yard was to break up block trains into sections for private firms and for the nearby Grimethorpe Depot. It had a capacity of 4,000 wagons daily over the hump.

WHITEMOOR YARD

Focus on Freight

Right: **A Speedlink train prepares to leave Whitemoor *en route* from Wisbech to Glasgow Deanside on 25 August 1985.** *P. Wakefield*

Right: **The Up Yard at Whitemoor was still busy on 13 January 1981 — although a slight mishap seems to have occurred!** *Paul D. Shannon*

Right: **Class 31 No 31227 departs with a coal train for Mansfield Concentration Sidings on 13 January 1981.** *Paul D. Shannon*

Eastern Region

Left: **The disused hump in the Up Yard in January 1981. The entire yard would be closed within a decade. BR later sold part of the redundant yard space to the government for the building of Whitemoor Prison.** *Paul D. Shannon*

Select Bibliography

Allen, G. Freeman; *The Eastern Since 1948*; Ian Allan, London 1981

Allen, Geoffrey Freeman; *British Railfreight Today & Tomorrow*; Jane's Publishing Co. 1984

Anderson, P. Howard; *Regional Railway Handbooks No. 1: The East Midlands*; David & Charles, Newton Abbot 1986

Baker, S. K.; *Rail Atlas of Great Britain & Ireland*; Oxford Publishing Co., Yeovil 1988

Batty, Stephen R.; *Rail Centres: Sheffield*; Ian Allan, London 1984

Body, Geoffrey; *Railways of the Eastern Region*; Patrick Stephens Ltd., Wellingborough 1989

Coles, C. R. L.; *Railways through London*; Ian Allan, London 1983

Collins, Michael J.; *Freightliners*; Oxford Publishing, Yeovil 1991

Conolly, W. Philip, & Vincent, U. A.; *British Railways Pre-Grouping Atlas & Gazetteer*; Ian Allan, London 1976

Davies, R., & Grant, M. D.;*London and its Railways*; David & Charles, Newton Abbot 1983

Joby, R. S.; *Regional Railway Handbooks No 2: East Anglia*; David & Charles, Newton Abbot 1987

Mitchell, Vic; Smith, Keith; Awdry, Christopher; & Mott, Allan; *Branch Lines Around March*; Middleton Press, Midhurst 1993

Saunders, John (ed); *Lincs, Notts & Derbyshire by Rail*; Jarrold Colour Publications, Norwich 1990

Waszak, Peter; *Rail Centres: Peterborough*; Ian Allan, London 1984

Also various issues of *Modern Railways* and *Railway Gazette*.